DO NOT REMOVE
CARDS FROM POCKET

ALLEN COUNTY PUBLIC LIBRARY

FORT WAYNE, INDIANA 46802

You may return this book to any agency, branch,
or bookmobile of the Allen County Public Library.

DEMCO

**Protecting Information in
The Electronic Workplace:**
A Guide for Managers

Protecting Information in The Electronic Workplace:
A Guide for Managers

JAMES A. SCHWEITZER
Systems Security Technology Manager
Xerox Corporation

Reston Publishing Company, Inc.
A Prentice-Hall Company
Reston, Virginia

Library of Congress Cataloging in Publication Data

Schweitzer, James A.
  Protecting information in the electronic workplace.

  Bibliography: p.
  Includes index.
  1. Computers—Access control.   2. Electronic data
processing departments—Security measures.   I. Title.
QA76.9.A25S363   1983   658.4'78   83-9573
ISBN 0-8359-5702-0
ISBN 0-8359-5703-9 (pbk.)

Copyright 1983 by
Reston Publishing Company, Inc.
A Prentice-Hall Company
Reston, Virginia 22090

10   9   8   7   6   5   4   3   2   1

Printed in the United States of America.

7073543

To Millie Jane
(NHATAMB)

Contents

Foreword

"Oh well, another Monday morning. Unlock the door, hang up my coat. Now, turn on the lights, turn on the microcomputer, the printer, the intelligent modem. Unlock my file drawers, get out the disks . . . let's see, which ones do I need this morning? Probably the systems disk for word processing. Have to write those memos about arrangements for the meetings in California. Load in the two disks, the systems disk, and the one with my correspondence files. Now, first of all, I must check my mail. Make proper key entries on my microcomputer keyboard. What do you know—I have finally heard from Charles in Europe about that trip. I'd better print that out. And here is a report on an electronics theft—have to put classified information markings on that one, and print it for the boss to see. Send a reply to confirm receipt. Now to write those memos. Then later, I must load the sort programs and work on those contacts files. And I have to send a message to Paul—he should meet me at the airport tomorrow. He'll have the message in a few minutes. No need to encrypt—that message can be sent in the clear. More mail . . . Here's a report I must review and I can 'sign off' on it using the communications system—no need to generate paper. I think I'll get some coffee . . ."

Not a far-fetched scenario today. This book addresses a new and critical dimension in the use of computers in business—automation at the personal workplace, at the office, and at home.

Not too long ago, for the average business manager "security" was concerned solely with the direction of a guards force, with responsibility to maintain safety and security within plants and offices. With the startling increase in so-called "white collar crime" and the rise of international terrorism, business security must include a wide range of subjects. Special training courses on hostage negotiations, fraud detection, and computer systems security are popular and illustrate a recognition of this enlarging responsibility.

In some companies the senior security executive is titled "Risk Control Manager," based on the classic risk management approach. Essentially, this approach recognizes that all business activity entails risks and that these risks cannot always be avoided but may be controlled through good management.

The risk management process envisions a selection from alternatives:

1. Deciding to control or minimize risk through application of security elements, which we describe here as physical, procedural, and logical (the "security" function).

2. Changing operational practices so as to eliminate risks, such as changing a product formula if a component material is explosive.

3. Seeking to minimize risk of loss through the purchase of insurance—actually a sharing of risk with other policyholders.

4. Making a decision, after analysis, to bear a risk as a part of doing business.

This process offers a realistic basis for assignment of the resources devoted to security. Having a broad management view of business, the professional manager is ready to address the vulnerabilities of business operations in the 1980s, recognized by many as the "information age." (The term "information age" refers to the use of computers to provide information as a common resource—much as electric power is available. Some people have predicted that we will soon be able to "plug into" computer power just as we now can plug into electric power and the telephone system. The proliferation of home terminals, the rapid expansion of business (and government) data bases, and the current ubiquity of microcomputers in business support this thesis.)

Management experts are agreed that the critical resources of today's businesses include:

- Plant and equipment
- Employees
- Liquid assets (cash, receivables, inventories, and supplies), *and, of growing importance,*
- Information

The professional manager will consider information as a critical resource for any competitive business and will

1. Recognize the important information elements used in his or her company.
2. Evaluate these information elements so as to be able to place proper security elements and offer imaginative alternatives should costs militate against "book" solutions.
3. Understand how these information elements are developed, controlled, and processed (the "information management" process).
4. Participate in systems installation decisions to ensure that required security elements are provided.

Exhibit i–1 illustrates the responsibility set and security element responses.

We must be especially concerned with the process for the delivery of information to the business activity, found in the automation of the office and professional personal workstation. Data center security issues have been well addressed in most businesses, but in workstation automation we have a new and more challenging matter. Not only is the information delivery and processing environment more complex, but the information involved is also of a different quality, requiring more care and more precise handling.

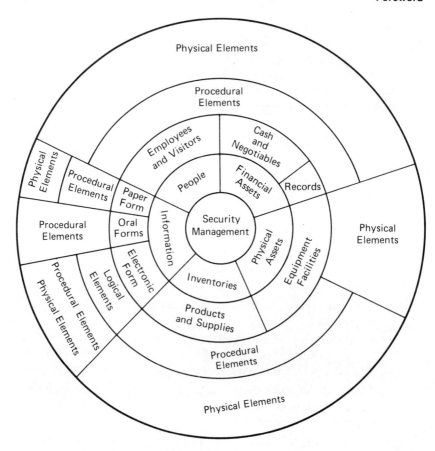

EXHIBIT i–1. Business resources, security management responsibilities, and application of security elements.

This book, then, is about this new responsibility. We will look at the developing personal computing world, at work and at home. We will see why information is becoming a critical resource that needs protection. And we will suggest how you, the professional manager, can go about protecting your information in this exciting environment. The information age is here.

1

Revolution in the Hundred-year Office

The white-collar robot. The literature on the electronic revolution in the office grows daily, and each technological breakthrough unleashes avalanches of glossy booklets from the vendors, pushing the advance guard of machines into the new electronic office. The "miracle chip" has moved into the office largely in the form of the microcomputer. These desk-top machines have brought computers out from under the strict control of data processing departments and made them readily accessible to the end user. They draw their advantages from the microprocessor that is their brain—they are portable and cheap, and they consume small amounts of power. These qualities of the microprocessor have led to the concept of distributed data processing (DDP).

Lynn M. Salerno[20]

Consider the business office of recent times, perhaps 1975. In the methods, equipment, incidentals, and terminologies used, there has not been much change since 1875—a hundred years! All the "essentials" for operation of the business office were designed for handling pieces of paper. The business lexicon contains words intended for the paper-oriented communications system. To most people, the words *memo, letter, message,* and *file* all mean pieces of paper. Then there are the in-box, out-box, reference file, calendar, telephone message note, file cabinet, notebook, folder—all about pieces of paper.

Our supply of terms is so tradition-oriented that designers of new systems must either adapt old terms to new meanings—as when a logical or electronic message is called a "memo"—or must come up with painful substitutes—for example, referring to the act of using a pushbutton telephone as "punching."

There have been two significant changes in the process of dealing with business communications (the primary function of knowledge workers). The first was the telephone, about one hundred years ago. Although many small improvements have been made, the phone is still used in the original way in most cases, that is, by using a hand-held instrument. Videophone and other advanced products (speaker phone, "system" telephones) have not yet come into general use. The wrong-number, not-here-now, will-call-back problems are still with us after a century. (Other trivia about the office: pencil with eraser tip, 1858; fountain pen, 1888; typewriter, 1927.)

The second major change was the introduction of the plain paper copier, which eliminated the need for tedious retyping, use of carbons, or preparation of stencils, and allowed transmission of paper-based information in parallel. That is, a memo writer could now send the memo to twenty people and assume they would all get the message at about the same time, as compared to serial delivery of an original via the old "routing slip."

Now the office workplace is being affected as never before by the electronic revolution, thought by many to be, in effect, the equivalent of the industrial revolution of the last century. To understand the security implications of personal workplace automation we must have a good grasp of what is happening and what the new systems can do. Because we need a term to cover all the various types of systems used in automating the personal workplace (and can't find one in current literature), we will use "personal workstation automation" or "PWA."

Our term "PWA" covers all applications of computing power at the personal workstation level. At the end of this chapter, a glossary of terms defines some commonly used PWA designators. Chapter 5 describes several PWA systems; many others exist, and more are announced almost daily.

The information explosion of the past twenty-five years has been the result of new technology developments, which have resulted in our ability to promulgate information about the technology itself. Hence, the explosion of information feeds on itself, the existence of information technology encouraging and enabling people to work ever more efficiently on developing newer and better systems.

PRODUCTIVITY—THE DRIVER

The greatest opportunity, and possibly the greatest need, for productivity improvement in American business can be found in the "white collar" arena. Well over 50 percent of the workers in this country produce and process information rather than material goods. It has been estimated that the direct cost of office operations in 1979 exceeded $800 billion in the United States. It is predicted that this figure may rise as high as $1.5 trillion by the end of the decade.

American Productivity Center[19]

A startling change in the way we do business is under way. Specifically, this change affects those of us who are "knowledge workers," who work at desks, laboratory tables, and drawing boards, and who process information rather than working to change physical matter location or form. Usually, the most evident of the many facets of this rapidly occurring evolution in business practice is in the office, e.g., the "automated office," "word processing," "office information systems—OIS." Unfortunately, while those terms have popular acceptance, they are too narrow for appreciation of what really is happening, which is the application of computing power at the personal level, at work and at home. This automation of the individual workplace has staggering implications, some not understood fully, and others not yet recognized. Among these effects of personal workplace automation (or PWA) is a subtle but most critical need for rethinking of the traditional practices and measures for ensuring the security of a key business asset, information.

The exact nature and ways of implementing this developing change in the practices of knowledge workers is yet unclear. Some impressive pieces of hardware and parts of systems are on the market and in use, while many more exciting concepts and systems are in development.

Several aspects of PWA are already obvious and may help us to perceive more clearly what is happening or what may happen in the near future.

- Personal workstation automation is a development of the generic traditional computing environment and not a separate phenomenon (see Chapter 7). As we shall see, communications is the essence of the knowledge worker's activities. The new information systems achieve optimal value in terms of productivity contributions when they allow efficient communication with the already developed large information data bases in central data centers. Our conclusion from this fact must be that a stand-alone PWA system is, in most cases, not as effective in helping the knowledge worker as it could be if it were connected to other systems, especially those with large information stores. Effective information access controls will be critical.

- As it develops in both contents and applications, PWA will offer a bewildering and sparkling array of capabilities. In addition to the basic information record creation, storage, retrieval, and processing (those things the big computers have always done well), PWA will provide us with electronic message or "mail," personal calendar scheduling, word processing, end-user application development, facsimile transmission (you could send a picture as well as a letter!), and teleconferencing (which could eliminate the need for many business trips). As you probably have noticed, most of these attractive features involve communications. Users will want to be able to specify who can connect with these services, for both privacy and cost control purposes.

- Not only is PWA changing *how* we do our jobs, but it is changing *what* we do. In other words, both job content and organizational structure will be modified as PWA is absorbed into the business mainstream and eventually affects all knowledge workers. James Martin, in his seminar "The Office of Tomorrow" says, "Administrative patterns in a paperless office should be totally different from today." Auditability and security built into paper-oriented systems must be replicated in PWA.

Some early applications of PWA have already become de facto standards, for example, the use of word processing machinery by secretaries. In research, we see the widespread use of professional workstations, such as the ten-year experiment with the "Alto" processor at Xerox's Palo Alto Research Center.[1] However, it is not yet clear on a broad scale just how PWA will be applied and what its effects will be.

From stories in newspapers and technical journals, we can see what the pundits think on this subject (paraphrased by the author):

> An assistant secretary of transportation can push a button on the computer keyboard on his desk and see his daily calendar on a television-type screen. He can look at calendars of subordinates, too. When completely installed, his system will allow him to peruse timely staff memos, fire off messages in reply, and enjoy services which combine the utility of a doodle pad, telephone log, card file, and filing cabinet. Since the system will be lightweight, he can take it home at night or along on business trips.
>
> *(Bernard Wysocki*, Wall Street Journal, *July 6, 1979.)*

> We will soon have a basic new tool which will allow us to break the habit of "follow me" solutions and will enhance creative problem solving across the spectrum of human affairs. This device will take information processes beyond the computing centers to every person in every walk of life, and will perform dozens of functions not available today. It will be an "intelligent associate" that each person can rely upon to enhance individual performance.
>
> *(J. Thomas Markley*, Telecommunications, *September, 1979.)*

> Computing will become distributed, like it or not. Tied into a communications network, the (PWA) machines provide versatility. The fundamental economy of microcomputing will cause the distributed processing revolution to occur. Micros are changing the rules for computer price/performance and many applications can run satisfactorily and cheaply on a small machine. Machines such as the Xerox 820 are referred to as "desktop workstations."
>
> *(Lois Paul, quoting John Landry of*
> *McCormack & Dodge Corp.,*
> *Computerworld, November 2, 1981.)*

The evolution, or perhaps revolution, of the personal workplace is being driven by competitive pressures for productivity improvements across the total workforce. The United States now has about 50 percent of the work force engaged in knowledge work. Yet investment in the facilities provided to knowledge workers has been only one-eighth that of investment in factories, and as a result, factory productivity has increased markedly over ten years while office productivity remained static. Office (knowledge) workers are undercapitalized. Paul Strassmann of Xerox says, "As you give each 'white collar' worker a personal workstation—his or her own equivalent of (investment in) a passenger car—we believe that by 1990 the 'office equipment' category will be about $10,000 per white collar worker." Exhibit 1–1 shows current capitalization for various kinds of workers.

EXHIBIT 1–1
Are Office Workers Undercapitalized?

	Installed Value Per White Collar
Office Equipment	$ 800
Computers	$ 4,400
Telephone	$ 6,000
Office Furniture	$ 1,500
Office Space	$12,000
	$24,700

Source: Paul Strassmann, Xerox Corp.

With human labor costs escalating steeply and a growing majority of workers in the white collar and service industries, startling improvements in the cost/benefits equation for electronics makes microcomputing a key opportunity for providing value-added efficiencies to knowledge workers. In some cases, PWA will supplant or displace human labor, thus offering tremendous leverage for productivity gains.

An example of the pressure for improvement in knowledge worker productivity can be seen in the chart in Exhibit 1–2, showing that about $300 billion in office worker costs could be saved were PWA applied.

The attractiveness of microcomputers as a value-adding investment or as a replacement for human labor is illustrated in Exhibit 1–3, which portrays the cost/performance evolution of computer hardware over 30 years. A simplistic projection of this development leads one to conclude that computing services will

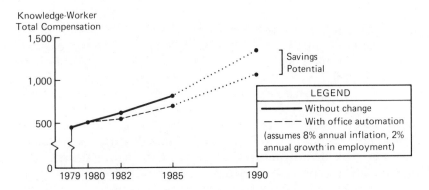

EXHIBIT 1–2. Potential Savings from the Application of Office Automation (adapted from productivity estimates of Booz · Allen & Hamilton Inc., New York)

become as cheap and as available as electricity. PWA is the delivery medium for these services.

The major thrust of this development of computing technology may not be towards continuing cheaper hardware but rather into alternative and new applications. That is, microcomputers will appear in all kinds of products for use in business and the home. Among the applications that may be considered as PWA are computerized telephone sets, automated paper (mail) delivery,

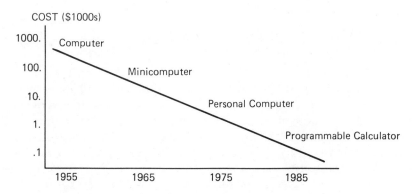

EXHIBIT 1–3. Cost for Equivalent Computing Power.

full function hand-held programmable calculators with communications, and interactive executive-secretary processors.

The basis for the development of microcomputing technology, which in turn is the core of PWA, is the "very large scale integrated circuit" or VLSI. In each year since industry began
producing integrated circuits (about 1960), the number of functions, or electronic pathways, per "chip" has doubled from that of
the previous year. By 1980, almost 150,000 elements could be
placed on a chip the size of a postage stamp. Manufacture of such
minutely detailed structures depends on computers, and more
specifically, on computer-aided design. Thus, the microcomputer
business depends on its own products for further design and
manufacture of increasingly efficient and smaller products. VLSI
provides systems builders with several inherent characteristics
that are the keys to continuing development and application of
PWA. These characteristics are

1. Reduced cost for electronic components. Since 1950, the
   cost of an electronic element has been reduced to 1/1000
   its original price.
2. Increased reliability. These components are 100,000
   times more reliable based on mean time to failure.
3. Smaller size. Size has been reduced, illustrated by the
   ubiquitous calculator now an essential part of every person's kit.
4. Increased efficiency. VLSI uses less energy and produces
   less heat, thus allowing simple product design and installation. (From John S. Mayo, Bell Laboratories,
   "VLSI": *Computerworld*, Vol. 14, No. 25, June 23, 1980.)

Technology development thus ensures the application of
PWA, although we are not certain exactly how this will affect overall business operations. The applications will be extensions of the
now-routine use of electronics for handling information.
Microelectronics will extend man's intellectual work power just as
investments in equipment extended his physical powers in the industrial revolution.

The business manager must understand these exciting developments and must recognize how they will affect the security of
the business information of his or her company. The chapters following provide such an understanding and will propose ways for

the manager to ensure continuing protection for information while enjoying the benefits of personal workstation automation.

GLOSSARY OF TERMS

The newness of our subject requires that we take time to understand the meaning of terms used in our discussion of personal workstation automation and security.

PWA or Personal Workstation Automation: A general term that covers the various units and systems now on the market which automate previously manual knowledge worker functions. Among the various PWA systems are

> **OIS or Office Information Systems:** Systems which provide electronic secretarial, managerial, or professional services.
>
> **Office Automation Systems:** Same as OIS.
>
> **Professional Workstations:** Microcomputer-based processors for document creation, graphics, computing and communications.
>
> **Management Workstations:** Similar to professional workstations.
>
> **Word Processors:** Workstations specially designed for efficient document creation, e. g., "typing and filing" work.
>
> **Servers:** Devices which provide special services to network-connected PWA systems. (Example: a file server which manages disk files for system users.)
>
> **Image Processors:** Microcomputer systems which handle documents as images rather than as discrete series of characters, i. e., as a picture.

Security Elements: Constructs of the basic security methods, such as door locks, passwords, guards, cabinet locks, magnetic card keys, access control programs. Security elements are viewed to be in three categories or levels: physical, procedural, and logical.

Security Levels: A grouping of security elements according to their characteristics. Generally, it is convenient to consider three levels: physical, procedural, and logical. Elements from the three levels are often interchangeable and thus offer a certain flexibility in assignment. (Logical elements include computer software or programs, computer and electronic hardware, and the use of these elements, e. g., entering a password.)

Knowledge Workers: Anyone working outside the manual categories where the work consists of changing physical attributes; anyone whose primary task is the handling or processing of information. In other words, managerial, clerical, and professional workers, including scientists, engineers, consultants, authors, designers, artists, medical doctors, graphics designers, lawyers, and accountants.

Network: Any set of devices or systems connected by wires or radio to allow interchange of information.

Communication: The act of using a network.

Database: A collection of interrelated files, typically used by varied functions, e. g., a customer data file used by order processing, marketing, billing, accounts receivable, etc.

Local Area Network (LAN) or Campus Network: A network connecting computer devices within a building or among neighboring buildings, usually not more than 1000 meters apart, and usually having high data flow rates (three to ten million bits/second).

Logical Security: Software programs that control access to information in process or in storage in computer systems. Such programs may allow the use of passwords or other identification for purposes of user identification, authentication, and authorization. Also, logical security systems assist in procedural activities such as monitoring computer use. Includes transformation or encryption of information.

2

Information—the Critical Business Asset

In modern society, information is power, and broad access to information services and products is a key requirement to preserve democratic processes and prevent domination by technocrats and other information elites. The extent to which information is defined as a public or private good (or some combination thereof) will greatly impact upon the relative roles of the public and private sectors and upon the institutional forms involved in the information infrastructure.

Dordick, Bradley, and Nanus[21]

Personal workstation automation (PWA) is important because it helps business knowledge workers function better; that is, PWA improves efficiency in processing of information. Today, such improvement is very critical as information has been recognized as one of those assets necessary to a successful business.

All assets must be protected or conserved if business is to continue successful operation, i. e., make a profit. The information asset becomes more important and, therefore, assumes greater value to its owner, as competition increases.

For a business with innovation-sensitive markets, information is the essence of survival. Any business offering products that apply technology must be very careful that research and

developments, marketing and pricing strategies, and business plans are kept confidential. Examples of indus-
must consider information as critical to success include automobiles, office equipment, computers, pharmaceuticals, and some fashion goods. As with other assets, providing effective protection requires that the business first determine asset values. No insurance company would write a policy based on indefinite value.

We should look briefly at the evolution of information forms. Originally, and probably in the middle ages, writing was extremely costly because so few people were literate and paper was expensive. Most business depended on barter, and we may assume that many "deals" were on the basis of an oral agreement. Recently, a newspaper article told about research into numbers found on the city walls of Avignon, France, which turned out to be numbers chiseled by the stonemason who built the wall, to ensure payment from the town fathers! Once paper and writing came into common use, professions such as accounting became practical, and business information took on its first change of form. A third form of information, signals, appeared at some later date, probably in the course of military development. A fourth form was similar to signals, but it involved electrical current and was called *telegraphy*. The telegraph appeared in the mid-nineteenth century and became extensively used for business purposes, right up to the current times. The telephone added a fifth form, using analog signals. Finally, the digital computer provided the most important new form since printing.

Electronic information appears in two modes, as analog tones (or beeps) in message transmissions, and as digital signals (off or on) as when written on disks, tapes, or cartridges as storage media, or in computer core during processing. Electronic digital forms will gradually replace older electric signal forms as digital telephone message systems are installed.

In addition to having very few time or space constraints when in a network environment, electronic information forms can be condensed and can be processed with great speed. Relatively small disks that will contain an entire filing cabinet of information in the space of a cigar box are under development. A recently announced large computer, the Cyber 205, has a processing speed of 800 million operations per second.

Enhancing the technical attractiveness of electronic information forms is the economic benefit. Professor Edward Fredkin of MIT says that it is now cheaper to maintain a reference book on magnetic media, making it available via electronic reference, than it is to keep the book in the traditional library.

The rapid application of the computer as a business tool, especially in PWA forms, means that managers must be thinking about the impact of technology on the security of the business information asset *now*.

VALUING INFORMATION

Information values may be conceptualized either subjectively or objectively. A subjective valuation addresses the intrinsic matter of information. The business could identify information groupings such as "research information," "personnel information," or "financial information." Obviously, there might be dozens of such categories. An objective valuation views all business information in light of its importance to meet requirements of continuing operability, law, or charter. Objective valuations, therefore, might be "operational information," or that data necessary to continue profitable business activity, and "archival information," or that data necessary to ensure business continuity or compliance with law.

These objective and subjective information value groupings can be used singly or in combination in a business program that might be called "information management," or "information resource management." Although we are primarily interested in the security of business information in the electronic age, we should understand that information management is a broad and important subject.[3] Information management can be viewed as a high-level responsibility that includes

- Data base management
- Information systems management
- Information processing resource (hardware) management
- Communications systems management
- Records retention programs
- Information security and recoverability programs
- Office systems management

Information management and data administration result naturally from a recognition that data must be managed the same as capital, equipment, and other resources of business. Information is "a crucial commodity in a corporation's attempt to compete in the open marketplace." Within the business, information will become a resource for which groups will compete—unless multiple copies are maintained, which presents problems of currency and concurrent updating.[2]

In most businesses today, these responsibilities are shared among several senior executives, but in the future we will see more centralization of these functions in recognition of their importance. Perhaps a more basic reason for establishing an "information manager" at a senior level is that this most important asset, information, is really one entity which appears in many forms. In terms of information systems, including PWA, it is essential that business ensure consistency of information definition, application, and control across the many users who will access the company's data bases.[29] Most larger businesses have managers responsible for controlling information in computing systems application through the use of data dictionaries and other software which allow practical control, ensuring consistency and relative ease of use. With the implementation of PWA, businesses face a proliferation of information elements which, if not controlled, could lead to chaotic welter of thousands of information files, each with an individual interpretation or definition.

The process of information valuation, then, is a part of the larger scheme, "information resource management" (IRM), which is critical to effective business use of information in the coming years.[28] As the manager goes about the task of preparing for the use of PWA, he or she must coordinate with the appropriate information management functions in the business. Exhibit 2–1 shows the necessary relationships between security and information management activities.

Good information valuation, whether on an objective, subjective, or combined basis is necessary for effective information security practices. Also, information valuation can assist in other information management activities, such as data base design, records retention scheduling, and recoverability (contingency) planning. Information valuation provides the business with definitions of the relative values of its information. For practical security purposes, the valued information must be grouped or designated as to the appropriate protective rule sets. Such designation is usually called "classification." Examples of such groupings are the government use of terms like "secret" and "confidential." In-

EXHIBIT 2–1
Security and the Information Management Function

Function	Security Management	Information Management
Information valuation	Guidance on policy	Policy compliance
Information retention and storage	Advisory	Sets Policy
Information systems design	Advisory	Directs
Information systems operation	Advisory	Directs
PWA hardware selection	Participates	Directs
PWA system design	Participates	Directs
Data definition	N/A	Directs
Data use authorization	Advisory	Authorizes
Information security practices	Sets policy	Advisory
Logical control systems	Advises	Develops

ternational Business Machines Corporation uses the terms "Registered IBM Confidential," "Confidential Restricted," "Confidential," and "Internal Use Only." Most large businesses in technology-related fields have established similar groupings.

These classifications refer to information valuations made on a subjective or objective basis and are the bedrock on which an information security program is constructed. Exhibit 2–2 illustrates the process (discussed below) of deriving a classification from the information valuations. In this case, we use both objective and subjective valuations to help in the classification decision.

In addition to objective and subjective values, a third decision element must be considered in a classification selection, that of risk. While the information valuation decisions, objective or

EXHIBIT 2–2
Development of Classification Decision

DECISION PROCESS

A Information Element	B Subjective Valuation	C Objective Valuation	D Risk	E Classification I = highest III = lowest
Financial summary	medium	low	high	II
Tax reporting	medium	low	low	III
Customer list	high	high	high	I
Personnel records	low	low	medium	III

DECISION RULES

Subjective	Value
Financial	medium
Marketing	high
Personnel	low

Objective	
Operational	high
Archival	low

Risk*	
Obvious exposure	high
Limited exposure	medium
Almost no exposure	low

*Risk due to handling process, inherent value, customary use, number of copies, or experienced losses.

subjective, deal with characteristics of the information itself or requirements for the information, "risk" addresses vulnerabilities evident in information handling, inherent values, processing, customary uses, or experienced losses. Finally, some information elements may be time sensitive, i.e., values change as time passes.

In Exhibit 2–2, four information elements are suggested in Section A. These are typical business data. For each, subjective, objective, and risk evaluations are made using the decision rules shown. These rules are developed to fit the business situation and many times are implicitly, not formally, applied. From the decision rules, valuations are entered in Sections B, C, and D. These valuations, considered together, form the basis for a classification selection (E). In the example, we use three levels of classification, the most common structure in business information valuation. Usually, the classifications are expressed as names, as in the IBM example, but for simplicity we use Roman numerals here.

The entire process in Exhibit 2–2 is somewhat judgmental, but it is fortified by the rationale of combining objective, subjective, and risk valuations, thus selecting a classification based on different, complementary aspects of the information and its use processes. All or any parts of the process could be modified or adapted to meet specific business circumstances, but the decision will include these elements in any case. The use of an explicit process helps ensure good decisions, and as we saw earlier, makes the decision process useful to other, related information management functions.

The classification of an information element determines the security measures to be applied. The definition of requirements for the protection of each selected classification requires business policies and operational standards, which are discussed in Chapter 4.

DIFFERING INFORMATION CHARACTERISTICS IN PWA SYSTEMS

The use of personal workstation automation affects the inherent value of the information because of the types of data that tend to occur in such systems. Traditional information systems, such as those processed on large computers in data centers, are now commonly taking the form of "databases" or large general-purpose collections of information (files) that are used by several business functions. An example of a file in such a database might be "customer name and address." The billing, shipping, receivables, credit, and advertising functions might all access this file. Another file in the database could be "account status," showing the debits and credits to the current date for each customer. These files illustrate the most common use of the computer in its traditional form—to collect information or data in some logical, orderly manner so that it may be referenced, sorted, and collated for business purposes. Note that these collections of data may have inherent value. Certainly, a business would not want an "account status" file made public, if only because it would tell competitors who the best customers are. But the management conclusions drawn from analysis of reports generated from the business database are not stored in the computer but rather are a result, probably in written (paper) form, of a study of summaries of the computer data.

Professor Leslie Ball of Babson College, a specialist in computer security, addresses this distinction:

> Computer systems tend to store data, while (PWA) systems usually store information. Data is a collection of facts, while information results from the massaging, or processing, of data into a form useable for management decision-making. For example, the computer system might contain a record of all sales for the last year. When we process that data to determine the sales trends, we are producing valuable management information. It is that information which we most often find in memos from sales managers located in (PWA) systems.[14]

Here is where the difference in information characteristics occurs when personal workstation automation (PWA) is put into use. PWA is a medium where "decision information" is stored and used. The PWA system may be used to withdraw data from a central database and then to process it so as to arrive at a decision form. Or PWA files can contain individually entered pieces of information from reports that the user is studying. This information may then be processed to arrive at a decision-level file or document. Note the difference in the quality of the data. Usually, data from the central database must be analyzed before useable information can be obtained. Information from PWA systems may already be in "decision form." In other words, the data has already been analyzed; a decision has been made, and the information file may indicate a strategic direction, product development option selection, or other critical business intelligence. *The information found in personal workstation automation systems tends to be more finished and hence more valuable.* Management consultant John Diebold puts our case succinctly:

> Information, which in essence is the analysis and synthesis of data, will unquestionably be one of the most vital of corporate resources in the 1980s. It will be structured into models for planning and decision making. It will be incorporated into measurements of performance and profitability. It will be integrated into product design and marketing methods. In other words, information will be recognized and treated as an asset.[10]

3

Information Security Elements

Security measures for the protection of the business asset called information are, in many cases, the same as those for other assets. But because of the development of electronic information processing, special new protective measures have been created. For us to have an understanding of the modern information security environment, we shall review some basics of information protection and then discuss electronic information security technology, the esoteric and critical portion of our concerns.

All implementations of information security measures are based on information valuation, usually expressed in terms of a "classification." As a result of classification definition, access restrictions are established (policy) and means of enforcing these restrictions are provided (standards). Information access restrictions are of two types, subjective and objective. Subjective restrictions are based on the nature of the information itself. An example of a subjective restriction might be a rule which says that only certain senior payroll clerks may handle payroll records for people earning over $100,000 annually. The records (information) themselves then establish application of the rule. Objective restrictions depend on regulations established outside the information itself and usually fall into these categories:

- Information user's job assignment
- Information user's need-to-know
- Clearance by background check, etc.
- Combinations of the above

Subjective and objective restrictions are not mutually exclusive but rather tend to operate jointly, as in the example of the payroll clerk. While "need-to-know" is a good general rule on which to base information security, it is too general and susceptible to faulty definition. ("Joe is a nice guy, we should tell him.") As with information valuation, we want to be more specific and hence more technical in defining our restrictions.

Usually, authorization (the inverse of restriction) follows from application of at least two of the objective-type restrictions. The subjective kind of restriction is less common but is probably found wherever politically based or potentially embarrassing information is present.

Once restrictions are defined for each classification, the security manager can begin to build protective structures from the physical, logical, and procedural sets of security elements. The goal is to provide a security "cocoon" for each information classification that meets the needs of the business. As we shall see later, policy and standards help achieve this ideal level of protection.

In the electronic information age, protection will often require a combination of security measures from physical, logical, or procedural elements. In many instances, protection from one category may supplant another, and this may provide economies while maintaining essential security. We will see illustrations of this as we discuss policy and standards for information security.

THE SECURITY ELEMENTS

In the electronic age, information security measures may be conceptualized as physical, logical, or procedural. Definitions of the three types of security measures may be proposed as follows:

- **Physical:** Security measures that restrict physical access to a place or object. Examples include locked doors, motion detection systems, guards, vaults, and locked filing cabinets.

- **Logical:** Security measures that restrict access to information in electronic forms. Examples are software systems which implement access control through the use of passwords, fingerprint recognition, voice recognition, and transformation or encryption.

- **Procedural:** Security measures that provide administration of controls over authorization to see or use information. Examples include authorized employee lists, information element access approvals, coordination of hires and separations, monitoring of password use and change, and marking and mailing rules. Also, separation of duties, where one person must validate another's work, is another important procedural security element.

Since all business activities have physical aspects, physical security elements are almost always in use where personal workstation automation (PWA) is applied. Logical security elements are essential when information access restrictions are needed to apply to various individuals having access to computer files. This is almost always the case, since information communication is an important part of PWA. Procedural elements of security are traditional business control elements and have become even more important with PWA. As we will see in the cases (Chapter 9), procedural controls are necessary to ensure that logical security elements are maintained current with the business environment.

The information security standards for PWA must provide for flexibility in application, since the circumstances in which they must be applied vary widely. This flexibility is obtained by offering a "mix and match" set of security elements from the three security measure types—physical, logical, procedural. An example may clarify this.

In a situation where a central computer is permanently wired to several terminals, and only those terminals can access the computer, restrictions on information access may be achieved by any of the following methods:

- The computer files are protected by password access controls, and only the few authorized people are provided passwords. (Logical security element—passwords; procedural security element—maintenance of authorized employees list.)

- The terminals are placed in locked rooms, and only the authorized people are provided with keys. (Physical security element—locks; procedural security element—maintenance of key issued list.)
- The authorized users are provided with encrypted code magnetic stripe I.D. cards that must be entered into the terminal to sign on. (Physical and logical combination-encrypted cards; procedural element—maintenance of card issued list).

Note the importance of the procedural security element in each case.

To complete this section, let us consider a sample of the various security elements that might be found in each of the three security protection categories. Remember, these are to be used in combination in most cases and are generally substitutable.

Physical Security Elements

- Physical facility access controls—locks, doors, fences, etc.
- Facility access control systems—video monitors, electronic space monitoring systems, card key systems, etc.
- Guards and central security control facilities
- Document storage devices—files, safes, vaults, etc.
- Magnetic media storage containers—tape vaults, cabinets to hold disks, tapes, etc.
- Screens and partitions
- Document covers

Logical Security Elements

- Software (programs) packages to control central computer databases.
- Software to provided user-changeable passwords and other identification and authentication.
- Software to authorize specific action to individual identified and authenticated users.
- Software for encrypting information.

- Manufacturer-provided programs that allow file security to be established.
- Device identification-generating software and hardware.
- Hardware computer subsystems that maintain data integrity.
- Hardware systems that maintain network integrity.

Procedural Security Elements

- Maintaining lists of authorized systems users in current form.
- Monitoring reports of system security attempted violations.
- Coordinating employee job changes and separations to eliminate unauthorized computer access.
- Reviewing budget changes and computer use reports to look for improper uses.
- Reviewing "last password change" reports to ensure that users change passwords according to established procedure.

Note that many of these procedural elements can be accomplished automatically through computer matches and sorts. Security staff should not need to manually perform access list updates, etc., when such data is contained in digital form on other systems, such as personnel or payroll systems. The interface, for purposes of ensuring currency of access authorization records, should be automated, thus cutting administrative cost and improving effectiveness.

Readers wishing to have an understanding of the technical aspects of "logical" security should refer to Lance Hoffman's book, *Modern Methods for Computer Security and Privacy.*[5]

Application of the security elements is discussed in detail in Chapter 12.

4

A Structure for Information Security

pol-i-cy *n.* 1 **a.** prudence or wisdom in the managment of affairs:
SAGACITY **b.** management or procedure based primarily on material interest; **2.** a definitive course of action selected from among
alternatives . . . to guide future decisions.

Webster's Seventh New Collegiate Dictionary

We have noted that, in the world of PWA, the distribution of
computing power to personal levels means that each employee
must have awareness and motivation to comply with information
security practices. Ensuring security through supervision or en-
forcement audits becomes less practical as the capability for information retrieval, processing, and dispersal moves lower in the
organization. In addition, electronic information tends to lose the
time and space constraints normally associated with paper or
even, to some extent, oral communications.

Permeating an organization, especially a large one, with the
concepts of and interest in information security is no simple task.
One-shot efforts are unlikely to succeed as people tend to forget
quickly and will not, in any case, perceive information security as
an essential based on a single, or even a periodic, exhortation by
memo or speech.

EXHIBIT 4–1
SECURITY PROGRAM STRUCTURE

TOP LEVEL	POLICY (mandatory)
	statement of critical requirements

$$\downarrow$$

MIDDLE LEVEL	STANDARDS (mandatory)
	practices required to meet policy and ensure consistency
	among units

$$\downarrow$$

LOWEST LEVEL	PROCEDURE (optional if STANDARDS suffice)
	operating level instructions to implement standards

A well-conceived program structure is required. This structure might take on several forms, but the one recommended here has been used successfully in organizations of several sizes and is practical from a business viewpoint. That is, the structure must allow flexibility in terms of varying organizational goals within the overall business. And it must be perceived as reasonable in terms of cost measured against the business information vulnerabilities.

Very briefly, the recommended structure consists of four interdependent modules: (1) policy documentation, (2) implementation and modification, (3) maintenance, and (4) review. A detailed description of the development and real-life application of such a structure may be found in an earlier work, *Managing Information Security—a Program for the Electronic Information Age.*[16]

POLICY DOCUMENTATION

If a study were performed among major businesses to determine reasons for failures of security efforts, a prime candidate would have to be lack of expressed policy. Rather than discuss what should not be accepted in lieu of policy, we will concentrate on the characteristics of an effective business information security statement.

The policy, the bedrock of any security effort, must be

1. Published in the name of, or with the obvious support and agreement of, top management. To be realistic, policy must be
2. Stated in terms of minimal requirements only, so as to allow the flexibility of application required in a functioning business. Information protection processes in the electronic age must conform to practical business needs. Since practical application at the lowest organizational level is required for PWA, the policy must be
3. Supported by action documents that contain decision rules. These action documents can be called "standards" and can provide specific guidance to managers as to preferred courses of action under specified circumstances.

Note: A decision rule provides a standard reaction to a set of circumstances. Decision rules allow people to make consistent decisions that are in line with policy. For example, when high value information is present on any medium (paper, tape, disk), that medium must be protected in a manner consistent with the information value.

IMPLEMENTATION AND MODIFICATION

The second module is conceptual and organizational. It consists of a "network" of security people in each organization and at all significant levels. The full-time people, sometimes called "security professionals" or "security managers," are located at significant management levels in large organizations within the business. The part-time people, called "security coordinators" or "security monitors," help to maintain program awareness, motivation, and compliance with standards. (In some organizations, assignments as security coordinator rotate on an annual basis. After a number of years, there is a well-motivated, informed, and interested nucleus of people supporting the security program.)

This module is called "Implementation and Modification" because the network of security people is the means for these activities. Recall that the information security effort, in an age of per-

sonal workstation automation (PWA), must above all reflect the
needs and goals of the business. That is, the security measures
must not interfere with business activities. The means for
achieving a good fit is a continued sensitivity to ongoing,
changing business goals and procedures. The security
coordinator network provides the nerve endings to sense and react to changes in the business environment and to convey the
needs created by these changes to security managers.

PROGRAM MAINTENANCE

Our third module is called "Program Maintenance," and it deals
with on-going security activities. There are several parts to the
program maintenance module, including:

- Use of the second module (the security network) as a motivation tool and as a current operations review resource.
- Provision of training and motivational materials, meetings, and workshops.
- Continual evaluation of information security program
  content against changing business needs, with the security network serving as a "nervous system" for this purpose.

Note that each module depends on the next higher level module
for support. None can stand alone. In this third level, a series of
documents, concepts, procedures, and training activities, based
on the standards, is transmitted into the organizations using the
security network. Feedback on these elements, their applicability,
suitability, and effectiveness is via the network.

Elements from module one, then, are transmitted, applied,
and evaluated using module two. This overall activity makes up
module three.

PROGRAM REVIEW

This module follows naturally from the third. As the security
manager and staff visit the operating units or sites to provide motivation and training, they should also be performing security re-

view activities. These reviews are not audits—an important point. The "review" is an advisory consultation with unit or site security coordinators—resulting in comments and recommendations to appropriate management at unit or local levels.

Special security reviews, for example, concerning such things as logical access control implementation, computer hardware protection, or administration of information access authorizations, can be informative and helpful. Keep in mind that, per the first module, security is a business responsibility, and managers at all levels should welcome careful analysis of business vulnerabilities.

In addition to on-site visits, the security manager should be receiving regular reports about security activities and problems. Generally, the security manager should know about:

1. Unusual or serious problems. (If a problem is considered critical by top management, it should be reported immediately so that legal advice can be obtained and proper reaction developed. The definition of "critical" should be made when the program is developed.)
2. Spending plans.
3. Major objectives or special efforts.

Reporting frequency should be at least annually, with semiannual reports probably the best for any company of reasonable size. The security network, a mirror image of the business organization, provides the reporting channels.

5

Personal Workstation Automation Systems

We are no longer required to be astonished that the 100,000-to-1 price/performance improvement in computer systems power between the 1950s and today shrank both the physical size and the content of computers. Processors sometimes occupying 5,000 square feet or more of precious floor space and providing us with but a fraction of a MIP (million instructions per second) shrank to the size of a silicon wafer which, as an IBM ad proclaims, can pass through the eye of a needle. This provided a new dimension to our capacity to obtain computer systems power. Now we didn't have to visit a computer center or communicate with it from a terminal. The source became small enough to make it practical to bring the computer system to us—and carry it around.

From LSI silicon chips, whose elements vanish into the microscopic world, to massive networks, whose components span the continent, the sources of computer systems power may be tapped virtually at any time and at any place.

Charles P. Lecht[22]

Personal workstation automation (PWA) systems occur in many different forms, so it is not possible to point to a specific system and say, "That's it." A general definition might be "a system of connected computers and electronic information handling de-

EXHIBIT 5–1
Task Comparison

Traditional Office	*PWA System*
Step	
1. Ask secretary to get file for background.	Reference logical (electronic) files via desktop keyboard and video display.
2. Page through file and select relevant papers; mark up proper paragraphs.	Select proper paragraph and set aside in logical file (no paper yet).
3. Have secretary make copies of needed documents with marked paragraphs.	Not required; done logically in Step 2.
4. Write out memo, using cut-and-paste or rewriting to introduce information from file (by now lots of paper).	Key memo, introduce reference information from logical file by using system instructions (no paper yet).
5. Proof handwritten memo; make changes using arrows, crossouts, etc.	Proof keyed memo; make changes using edit features.
6. Give draft to secretary for typing.	Not required; print form created in Step 4.
7. Proofread finished memo and make changes.	Not required; done in Step 5.
8. Final typing.	If paper copy is needed, system printer creates same. Automated.
9. Copy.	Not required if addresses also have office system on network. Otherwise same.
10. Distribution—place in envelopes, address envelopes, mail. Lots of paper and paper handling.	Not required if addresses on network. Send out via address list from logical file. Little or no paper handling.
11. File copy.	Done via system to logical file.
12. Recipient wait 1 to 7 days for delivery	Delivery is immediate for logical "copies."
13. Replies received 2 to 14 days later if addressees answer on same day received.	Replies received as soon as recipients can answer if using system.

vices which delivers to the individual user at the workplace a combination of powerful capabilities tailored to his/her specific job requirements." (**Note:** Chapter 7 describes PWA systems, in terms of computer systems development, for those interested in a more technical view.)

Now, we can suggest the effect of PWA on a single task, that of creating and sending a business memo (Exhibit 5–1).

Although one can argue about the various steps and functions, it is clear that the automated process has about 50 percent fewer steps (12 versus 7) and gets the memo out to another person using the system in much faster time (seconds versus as much as seven days). There is also a marked security advantage, per se, in that it is possible to generate and file and deliver the memo without creating any paper. Assuming that adequate logical controls are in place to prevent unauthorized access to the memo, the absence of paper must be considered a plus. The vast majority of information security leaks in business (and government) are based on improper control of pieces of paper. However, as we shall discuss later in Chapter 8, there are new security concerns accompanying the benefits of a paperless workplace.

PWA SYSTEMS DESCRIPTIONS

A PWA system typically consists of

- A keyboard
- A visual display screen
- Computer memory
- Disk or tape magnetic storage for data

In some cases the PWA system also will have

- A printer
- Communications capability
- Central disk data store
- Capability to handle documents as "images"
- Other special capabilities, e.g., microforms, dictating

In terms of capabilities, units can range from a simple computer input/output terminal that uses a central computer for processing, to quite powerful individual computers that allow the personal workstation user to assemble information, process it, and prepare complicated output with graphics—and then to communicate that output electronically to a high-speed laser-driven printer thousands of miles away that delivers a high-quality document. Thus, PWA can complement all those things usually done by a knowledge worker and can make the individual more efficient and more effective through the power of the computer. Exhibit 5–2 shows the facilities potentially to be provided in an executive workstation.

An excellent example of a high-powered, professional-type personal workstation is the Xerox 8010. This device looks like a typical computer terminal with a video display tube and a keyboard. But it is designed to work with a network of other computers similar to the 8010 which offer information storage, communications within a high-speed local or slower-speed long distance networks, quality printing of documents, graphics, and "electronic mail" message services. Exhibit 5–3 illustrates this type of system.

EXHIBIT 5–2
Facilities in An Executive's Workstation

- Digital telephone with LED display.
- Telephone answering machine. Voicegram (speech mail) facility.
- Screen for receiving mail and messages.
- Word processing terminal in communication with secretary for change of words.
- Future speech input word processing machine.
- Videotext (viewdata) information system.
- Teletext facility (receives data broadcast on a television channel).
- Video tape player.
- Video tape camera over desk (for complex communication by engineers, scientists, or designers).
- Video access to local information room.
- Personal computing.
- Executive uses of computer terminal: mail and messages, information retrieval, database access, automated diary, automated in-basket work queue, action list, ability to place items on subordinates or other people's work queue, automatic follow-up, project status tracking, inspection and adjustment of mail typed by secretary before it is sent.

Source: James Martin, "The Office of Tomorrow."

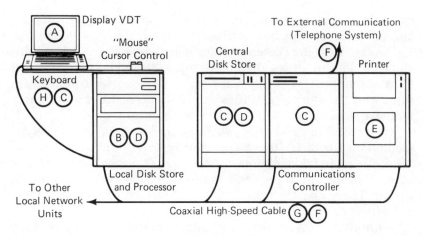

◯ SECURITY VULNERABILITIES SEE KEY

Security Vulnerabilities

A VDT display to unauthorized persons
B Media theft
C Unauthorized data modification, change, destruction
D Unauthorized access due to administrative control failure
E Document theft or unauthorized observation
F Unauthorized connections or taps
G Communications observation by unauthorized parties
H Unauthorized transmission

EXHIBIT 5–3. Personal Workstation Automation System: Professional Workstation.

It is a self-contained computing system that communicates with other devices on the network as required. It is completely human-engineered and offers a "mouse," a little device with wheels on the bottom which can be rolled about on a smooth surface (representing the screen) to move a cursor (an electronic pointer on the screen). Information files, documents, and other things stored in the system appear on the screen as "icons," representations of the physical objects used in "paper" systems. For example, a message being sent out is dispatched by pointing the cursor to a tiny "out box" picture.[9]

Along with the screen and keyboard, the basic 8010 unit includes a floor-mounted disk drive unit about the size of a small filing cabinet. Other units in the series that provide communications and file storage facilities are also about the size of small, half-size file cabinet. The printers are similar.

The local network (e.g., within a building or "campus"-type facility) for the 8010 uses a coaxial cable (the Ethernet). This cable is strung in false ceilings or other spaces, much like telephone cable. Connection to the cable is through a simple clamp-on connector. Therefore, the cable must be protected, if it runs outside of user-controlled areas, by encasing or burying.

Another PWA device is Digital Equipment Corporation's Rainbow 100 personal computer, which has a small keyboard and compact screen. Using a popular operating system software called CP/M, the 100 can operate as a stand-alone computer or as a smart terminal connected to a central database. It can also provide "electronic mail" services and has disk storage. A system like the Rainbow 100 would typically be used by a manager or professional to enhance information handling. (Exhibit 5–4 illustrates this category of PWA.)

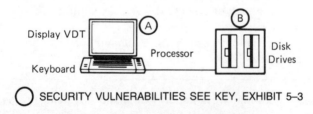

○ SECURITY VULNERABILITIES SEE KEY, EXHIBIT 5–3

EXHIBIT 5–4. Personal Workstation Automation System: Personal Computer.

A third example of the many types of PWA systems is the word processor, such as the NBI office automation units. Intended for secretaries or typists who handle light volumes of document preparation activities, the NBI units are about the size of a box of paper and serve a range of purposes. Many include a video display tube and keyboard, as shown in Exhibit 5–5.

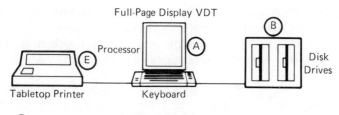

Full-Page Display VDT

SECURITY VULNERABILITIES SEE KEY, EXHIBIT 5–3

EXHIBIT 5–5. Personal Workstation Automation System: Word Processor.

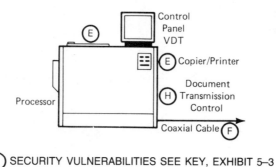

SECURITY VULNERABILITIES SEE KEY, EXHIBIT 5–3

EXHIBIT 5–6. Personal Workstation Automation System: Intelligent Copier.

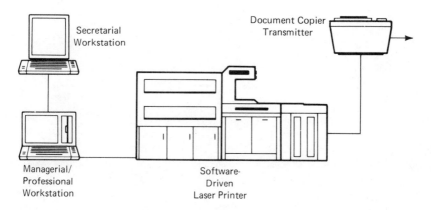

EXHIBIT 5–7. Personal Workstation Automation System Combination.

Other PWA systems include facsimile transmission systems (Exhibit 5–6), microfilm filing systems, automated typewriters, automated dictation equipment, or network combinations (Exhibit 5–7). Physical characteristics of this equipment are

- Size: bigger than a telephone, smaller than a filing cabinet.
- Placement: often on desktop, sometimes on floor.
- Weight: ten to one hundred pounds, approximately.
- Security: attractive to thieves, easy to move about, but in many cases so cheap as to be purchased as expendables.

6

Personal Workstation Automation Functions

(Businesses) have a select group of well-informed and powerful people who serve as their information gatekeepers. This information elite typically includes corporate controllers, strategic planners, brokers, lobbyists, and top executives privy to inside knowledge.

For this clique, executive workstations serve as a new and powerful communication medium. They provide instant access to specific organization members for the communication of sensitive and detailed information. They allow executives to bypass normal secretarial and corporate exchange channels. Confidentiality is more easily and completely ensured.

Managers can also have direct access to databases and personal electronic mailboxes through the use of a special function key at their workstation. Pertinent facts and figures that previously took hours or days to track down can be available to the user at the touch of a clearly labeled button.

James H. Carlisle[18]

It would be difficult, if not impossible, for someone who has never seen or driven an automobile to draw up practical traffic regulations. Similarly, managers must understand what personal workstation automation does, before trying to establish practical security measures.

As we discuss what PWA can do, it should be made clear that the computer power in these devices makes them very powerful and flexible. Because of this, a system user may develop new ways to apply the machine, ways which even the inventors and developers never thought about. Exhibit 6–1 provides a cursory list of PWA functions.

EXHIBIT 6–1
Personal Workstation Automation System Functions

System	Function
Automated copier	Copying
	Communications
	Filing
	Distribution of document
	Maintain lists
	Electronic "mail" server
Word processor	Prepare documents
	Generate "boilerplate" text
	Soft display proofing
	Text manipulation
	Global changes
	Automated editing
	Page set up/alignment
	Store information
	Communicate
Professional workstation	Prepare documents
	Prepare graphics
	Soft display proofing
	Mathematics, statistics
	Graphs, charts
	Information storage and retrieval
	Communications
	Message and mail systems
Personal minicomputer	Computation
	Filing
	Information retrieval
	Word processing
	Mathematics, statistics
Automated facsimile	Document distribution
	Automatic send/receive

Keep in mind that this is a very brief list and that the combinations of functions and product services are almost limitless.

PWA CAN COMMUNICATE

Communicating information is the primary mission of knowledge workers.[7] When we want to improve productivity, one of the first things to be considered is how to improve the efficiency of communications. The chart in Exhibit 6–2 shows that a large proportion of a knowledge worker's time (40 percent) is spent communicating, or trying to communicate. Exhibit 6–3 illustrates the proportional uses of time by white collar workers and shows the critical impact of automation on time-consuming activities.

PWA may allow almost instantaneous communications and avoid the delays inherent in using the mails or the telephone. PWA communications capabilities include:

- *Electronic mail:* The preparation, storing, and forwarding of messages via computer signals, usually over public wire and/or radio networks.
- *Facsimile transmission:* The copying, storage, and delivery of an image via computer signals (analog in past, now becoming digital), usually over public utility networks.

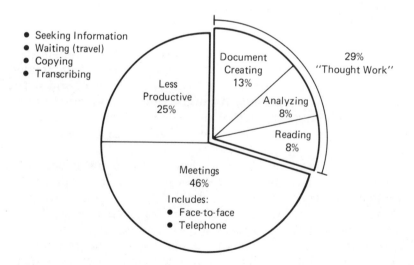

EXHIBIT 6–2. How Knowledge Workers Spend Their Time—By Activity (Courtesy of Booz · Allen & Hamilton Inc., New York).

EXHIBIT 6–3
White Collar Work Activities

	Professionals/ Managers	*Clerical/ Secretaries*
Text related		
Writing	27%	15%
Reading	12%	4%
Proofing, searching, filing	9%	7%
Dictating	2%	—
Verbally related		
Phone	5%	10%
Meetings	18%	9%
Equipment related		
Operating equipment	4%	18%
Calculating	4%	—
Other	19%	37%

Source: Paul Strassmann, Xerox Corp.

- *Voice message:* The recording, storage, and replay of voice messages using computer-controlled digital technology, usually via public networks.
- *Batch data transmission:* Preparation and sending of files, e.g., between word processors in digital streams.

Some of these messages and documents will be transmitted wholly within the office building or campus where the sender works. In those cases, the public utility network wire and radio connections do not become involved. However, in most cases, business communications that use electronic transmission media will travel outside local networks and thus go over public lines.

In some systems, interlocation message traffic will use "value-added networks," or VANs. These are services provided by suppliers who condition lines and resell services—the routing is still by public carrier wire or radio. The security managers should understand that there is really no such thing as a "private" or "leased line." That is, although one may lease a line from a communications company, the lease in effect gives one the right to the use of a pathway, or circuit, *not* a specific piece of wire or radio frequency. All the circuits, or pathways, go through the utility's (or the VAN's) switching centers, where the traffic is exposed to possible copying and analysis.

Informal networks established by clubs or hobby groups will become common as PWA systems are installed at work and at home. There are many concerns about such networks, including intrusion on other networks and systems to obtain information, to steal computer services, or to work mischief. Already, such cases are not uncommon (see Chapter 9).

There are also threats to individual privacy when individuals connected to networks (any use of a telephone computer connection) select services or products, perform financial transactions, or send messages. All of these data may potentially be observed or recorded for various purposes, some of which may not be in the individual's perceived interest.

People who have PWA systems may decide to create personal databases (this is almost a sure prediction, as witness the use of business telephones for personal calls and the ubiquitous computer-generated calendars, football pools, Boy Scout rosters, etc.), and this information pool may become available to many others (known and unknown) through intentional sharing with a group or through penetrations.

What we are going to face is a myriad of formal and informal networks, all using the "utility" or public network facilities. Although the formal or business networks may be assumed to have at least rudimentary logical security (perhaps an unreasonable assumption, in light of recent cases), all of these users will be physically connected at the telephone system switching centers. Immediately, we see a vulnerability to unintended cross connections or interception of radio signals and an opportunity for intentional penetration to other networks by skilled users, and thence to databases of individuals or businesses. (Chapter 9 describes some actual cases involving misrouting of critical data through network interconnect points.) Communication is a key element in PWA, but it also may represent a very real security problem, especially if external networks are connected.

The Automated PBX

An interesting aspect of personal workstation automation is the role that will be played by the telephone systems. With all its faults (it is among the least secure of communications modes), the telephone system is in a position to work tremendous leverage on any scheme to automate business activity. The presence of all the telephone wires and connections in every workplace and home represents an investment and a communications potential that cannot be duplicated.

In the near future, somewhat as a result of recent court decisions concerning the telephone companies, digital (computerized) private branch exchanges (pbxs) will begin rapid replacement of current equipment. This means that the pbx in a business, now used to switch connections among the various telephone extensions, will take on an additional role as a powerful local data network communications interface similar to the communications "servers" discussed earlier. The PWA units would be attached to the telephone wiring. This saves network installation costs. The impetus to use the pbx as a data communications controller is primarily economic—the wires and infrastructure are already in place. A disadvantage is that the twisted pair wires used for telephone circuits offer relatively slow data transmission rates. In addition to the in-building telephone wiring, the telephone system can offer good data services; often referred to as "value added" networks, specially conditioned lines may be leased which offer mixed data and voice capabilities at high speeds.

The use of the pbx as a communications controller for PWA systems has no special security constraints, provided the user can accept a physical connection with the rest of the world via the telephone network! However, it does require careful attention to the protection of telephone facilities, such as the room where the pbx itself is located, telephone wiring connection cabinets, trunk-carrying conduits, and so forth. Telephone facilities tend to be treated casually. They should not be. While visiting a data center, the author and a security manager were looking at a communications equipment room. A "scope" had been left attached by a telephone company repairman, and while we watched, a message went by reading: "1983 SPENDING PLANS ARE AS FOLLOWS; . . . ETC., ETC." Information that the business may want to keep private can quickly become public rumor if the telephone system is assumed to be secure. (See the encryption section in Chapter 11).

The Hyperchannel

Along with the potentially exciting uses for the automated branch exchange, the "hyperchannel" promises to change the information processing environment. In the past, many computers could not be connected because they spoke different languages. That is, the digital codes or the protocols used in the computers prevented users from connecting them together without expensive, and frequently difficult, modifications and software development. The hyperchannel allows computers made by different companies to be connected together on a single cable, thus permitting an exchange of information. Although the computers continue to speak their native languages, the hyperchannel translates everything into an understood format. The translation is done by a "black box" connected at each computer.

We have seen how personal workstation automation will deliver information and computing power to the personal level. Now, with the hyperchannel, we can see in the future the potential for a vast interconnected network, not only for smaller computers and PWA systems but also among the large database systems. Another interesting result of the development of the hyperchannel devices is that peripherals—the tape drives, disk drives, and printers usually attached to a computer—can now be placed more than a mile away from the central processor. The effects of central site security diminish in importance as we see computing power and information being more distributed. (See the various forms of distribution in Chapter 7.)

PWA CAN STORE INFORMATION

If one considers the typical office (or laboratory) environment, it is evident that considerable space and equipment are given to filing or storing information. Traditionally, information is stored away in printed form, and various methods are used to allow recovery of the information. Among others, documents are stored in creation date sequence, by subject, or by author, using folders, notebooks, file drawers, etc. PWA does away with the need for storing papers, at least insofar as the user and his correspondents have electronic information systems available. The second important PWA function, then, is information storage and retrieval.

Efficient PWA systems provide information storage methods that "look like" the traditional paper-oriented ways. That is, the system allows the user to store information locally, in his or her own "desk," or in a central file like the one maintained by the secretary or administrative assistant. In PWA systems, the local file is on a disk in the personal computing device. The central file is in a special computer station, sometimes called a "file server," which offers high capacity and which can be accessed by anyone on the connected networks. This dual filing arrangement, similar in concept to that used in the traditional "paper" office, has some interesting and serious security implications. The local or personal electronic file is usually provided with logical security controls. This means that only the immediate user or owner of the PWA system can access the information files stored on the disk in that particular device.

The central files, on the other hand, are often public files, unless specifically protected by the person establishing the files. If logical protection is not provided, anyone on the local or any connected network can access the information on the central files.

We cannot assume that acceptable information access controls are in place in either case. Sometimes, PWA users can set up local files and establish these as "public." In the case of the central files, the default is often to public status if the person establishing the files does not take specific action to provide logical protection. Some PWA systems may not provide built-in logical security, so the user must seek alternative (physical?) solutions.

Usually, in setting up electronic files on PWA systems, the user must: (1) determine the value or classification of the information, and then (2) establish suitable access control, usually by means of one or more authentications, typically passwords. Passwords, of course, should be changed periodically.

PWA CAN COMPUTE

So far, we have seen two important functions of PWA, namely communications and information storage and retrieval. A third important PWA feature is local computing. The PWA system may allow the user to retrieve information from several files, perhaps from distant places or apparently unrelated functions, and to process that information on the local (personal) computer. The resulting product may represent novel information, never before available, which may have high competitive or damage value. Information developed through combination or processing of files might include:

- Valuable research breakthroughs
- New information on the financial status of the business

- Market opportunities
- Solutions for technical product problems
- Business situation intelligence which differs from that publicly announced

The creation of this information is important because it is not occurring within the defined, established procedure typical of a routine business system. Financial analysts, for example, routinely make use of central databases via terminals. These activities are within a defined structure, schedule, and reporting sequence, and the central data center providing the services controls who may access the databases. The tests and analysis performed by the financial analyst are usually a repetitive, defined series of processes.

PWA may offer the analyst an opportunity to define and process against custom application programs that are created by the analyst himself. Also, PWA networking may allow the analyst to select from information databases maintained by others for other purposes. In some cases, the analyst may be able to access information which the "owner" would prefer that the analyst not have. This is not to pick on financial analysts, as there are large populations of knowledge workers in any large business who may be able to put together interesting, or dangerous, information conclusions by using the files of others. Consider the potential damage that could be done by personnel administrators, researchers, and, of course, computer security people (probably the worst case!).

Certainly one serious concern of management has to be the risk that, in using PWA systems to answer a strategic question, two skilled professionals will come up with conflicting answers because there is no standard definition of the many pieces of data being used. Hence, through subtle differences in input information or computer processing using "own" programs, results may be confusing or may provide misleading indicators for management.

PWA CAN CREATE SOFTWARE

A most important power of PWA is in the creation of software. Today most people using computer systems are taking advantage of software (or programs) written by professional programmers.

However, as systems demands become more interwoven with business needs and systems applications spread across all business activities, the use of professionals is becoming less satisfactory. This has happened because all of the "simple" applications, those which substitute the power of computing for routine clerical and administative tasks, have already been completed—jobs like general ledger accounting and payroll. The new demands are generally for shorter-term, more specific, needs that often deal with cognitive or rational processes. Management decision support systems are an example. These applications are difficult to program because the processes are hard to define, and the requirements may change suddenly and frequently. PWA, when the workstation is provided with a high-level programming language, will allow knowledge workers to program mini-applications to meet specific job needs. The benefits from such use of PWA devices are many. They include reduced costs (hardware costs going down versus rapidly escalating costs for programming); better systems response (PWA user knows requirements and does not have to explain to a systems analyst, who may not—and usually does not—get it all right); faster reaction to a need (schedule overruns are expected in the professional programming groups); and ability to make changes without a hassle about resources or timing. Users who do write personal programs to meet job information needs will probably use a language facility provided as part of the PWA system. The information processed by the user-developed program will probably come from the main databases of the business.[26]

Here we have a real quandary for information management and security management. That is, how can they encourage proper use of PWA by many employees and thus gain the benefits from increasing productivity while ensuring that information use is controlled both in terms of "who can see and do what" and "what information means" after unique processes in, perhaps, several places concurrently?

The first concern is one very close to traditional information security. The business manager wants employees to have all the information required to do an effective job but also does not want information to be unnecessarily spread about. The second concern refers to the dangers when a piece of information with supposedly common definition and valuation (or classification) is processed locally. Might the definition change, and will the users recognize that change? Will the classification change, and will the

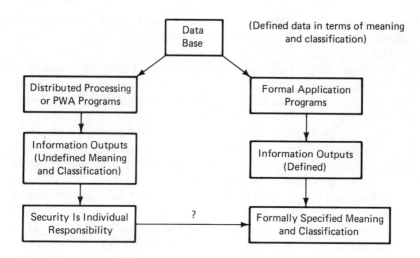

EXHIBIT 6–4. Spontaneous Information Generation *vs.* Traditional Generation—Security Aspects.

users react to that change with proper security? Exhibit 6–4 illustrates this problem.

SYSTEM INTEGRATION

The arrival of personal workstation automation on the computing scene has caused the issue of "systems integration" to become a topic of much discussion. Managers should understand in broad terms what this matter is about, since there are some information security implications in how it is resolved.[27]

Information processing has traditionally been accomplished through the use of relatively large computers situated in special facilities called "data centers." The distributed processing phenomenon, of which PWA is a form (see the discussion in Chapter 7), means that information can now be processed in many places by small pieces of computing equipment. These units may not be compatible in terms of computing mode, communications languages, or physical connections, thus making interchange of information a problem. As we have noted, communication of information among systems is one of the crucial advantages of PWA. Businesses would like to be able to conveniently transfer information from the large central databases in data center computers (called "mainframes") to and from the personal workstation (PWA) systems.

Generally, this is not yet possible in any consistent manner. Companies offering PWA systems have various network concepts that are intended to connect the information resources of a business in some cohesive manner. Since we want our valuable information to be protected (identified, marked, serviced) in a consistent and effective way, integration of the large computers with their databases and of the PWA systems with their smaller, decentralized files is a most desirable end.

Three different approaches to integration can be noted among the makers of PWA systems. IBM's approach has been to do all communicating through a mainframe computer in a data center. This is not surprising, since IBM's major business consists of selling and leasing mainframe computers. The data center then provides the systems intelligence for controlling the communications system or network. In the past, IBM has sold a number of competing products through different divisions—a practice that was somewhat confusing. Certain current products have communications capabilities with specific types of mainframe computers but not others. A recent IBM reorganization reflected IBM's determination to offer a really cohesive network service (which IBM calls SNA—System Network Architecture). IBM probably has the most comprehensive network connection offerings for various types of devices, but it stil has a way to go to "integration" of PWA with computer databases.

Wang Laboratories has proposed a fully integrated set of capabilities of information processing, connecting many resources, and providing many services. All the parts are not yet available, but the Wang approach is based on a set of technologies that Wang believes to be the important information processing capabilities needed for complete integration:

1. Data processing, the "mainframe" activity.
2. Word processing, the secretarial document creation function.
3. Image processing, the creation and communication of document images (as, for example, the professional workstation and "smart" copier/printer).
4. Audio processing, or telephone/video signals communications.

5. Networking, or interconnection of workstations and computers.
6. Human factors, the "friendliness" content of the PWA systems.

The Wang network uses a coaxial broadband cable which can carry all the functions; an implication that such a net will be costly and complex is difficult to avoid, although some experts believe it will be economical.

Xerox has begun deliveries of a baseband coaxial cable network called "Ethernet." Actually, the Ethernet is not necessarily a Xerox product at all but merely a coaxial cable to which many PWA units may be attached. Several other manufacturers (DEC, for example) also will provide PWA units for attaching to Ethernet. Further, connections to other networks, and thus to computer center "mainframes," can be made via units called "communications servers." Also available are file servers, print servers, and output printers, all of which connect to Ethernet through a simple clip-on connector. The Ethernet approach offers the user the opportunity (if many suppliers of PWA systems opt for Ethernet as a standard) to select various makers as suppliers while being assured of connectability and eventual integration.

Integration is an opportunity to build in information protection across several systems and locations, perhaps even across a worldwide network. Unfortunately, none of these manufacturers (at the time of writing) is supplying effective "total security" subsystems. But technically, the software capabilities of these PWA products can easily support security features, so we should be seeing some of these features over the next few years. A most important feature, for information security, will be hardware-based encryption to protect intersite communications.

7

Personal Workstation Automation— A Computer Perspective

The prime evidence of the information age, the automated personal workstation, is usually a form of "distributed" information system. Among several definitions of distributed systems are the following:

1. Distributed *Computing* System. A network of intelligent (i.e., can perform local processing operations under control of local programs) processors that share a common executive (or operating system). An example of such a distributed system is the Xerox 8010/Ethernet network, in which a series of identical computers perform various tasks, ranging from personal services to network control and file processing functions.

2. Distributed *Processing* System. A network of intelligent processors having more than one executive. This type of system may have several special-purpose programmable processors, such as communications controllers, database managers, and personal services terminals. In this case, these may be very different machines made by different manufacturers, and the only common ingredient may be the communications protocol which allows

interconnection. Banking networks and the management information networks of some large corporations are examples.

3. Distributed *Time-sharing* System.   A network of intelligent and/or "dumb" (not programmable) devices typically clustered around a large central processor, and which allow personal workstation users to share in the power and services of the central computer (or several interconnected computers). Business and research time-sharing networks are typical of this type of distributed system. Although most devices in such a system are nonintelligent, in some situations data can be drawn off the central computers for local processing.

4. *Stand-alone minicomputers* with or without terminal devices.   Although not technically a form of distributed system, the economics of computing indicate increasing use of minicomputers for special applications, as in manufacturing and research. For purposes of our discussion of security measures, we include this fourth category.

Most of the personal workstations and office information systems being installed in business today fall within one of these distributed system types. The key element in personal workstation automation is information communications. It should be noted, however, that many "personal computers" may not be connected to a network in the first stages of implementation. We may safely assume that eventually (within five years?) almost all computer workstation devices will be interconnected in some way; hence the definitions provided probably will have a very wide validity for our purpose here.

Some variations of these distributed systems, showing the automated personal workstations and other devices, are in Exhibit 7–1. There is almost unlimited potential for different combinations of devices and purposes within a distributed network, and several networks or different types of networks may be interconnected, probably through some public service, such as the telephone system or one of the value-added networks offered by service vendors.

Computing power appears almost as a continuum from formal setup with specific tasks in a fixed location to informal setup (portable device) for any task, in any location. Boundaries between types of computing have become blurred, and computer

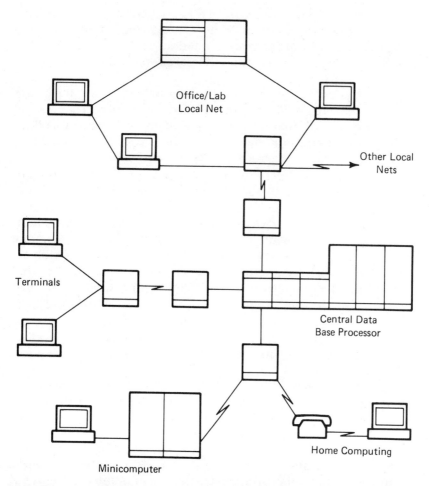

EXHIBIT 7–1. Distributed System Configurations (components have potential for unlimited variation in network layout, function, and intelligence).

equipment size descriptions now overlap to an extent which makes a term like "minicomputer" suspect.

We want to differentiate between traditional "batch" computing, where we used a large data center and brought information in paper form into and out of that center, and distributed computing, but with the latter there appears to be a range of hardware and functions that is difficult to specify.

Distributed computing in all its varied forms means that security considerations are different. The distributed systems environment differs from the traditional data center in several ways. For consistency, consider the levels of protection.

- *Physical level.* Computing equipment in a data center is consolidated and constrained within physical bounds, but distributed systems equipment is dispersed to both known and unknown places, and the hardware used covers a wide range of sizes, costs, and capabilities.
- *Procedural level.* Activity monitoring and general security control systems are mostly physical in nature in the data center, and user (authorized access) population is fairly well fixed. Distributed processing implies monitoring and control methods which allow for dynamic changes in user population, purpose, and information access, with a combination of centralized and decentralized security management of authorization and access control.
- *Logical level.* Software and hardware security elements in a data center are fixed but may vary widely across a distributed network. Effective control implies a high-level sophisticated approach.

As may be seen from Exhibit 7–2, combinations of security elements from various levels of protection are needed for the different computing environments. A proper combination of elements to suit the situation is critical and depends on the knowledge, skill, and judgment of the security manager. In the myriad forms of distributed systems, the concentric levels of protection apply. From each level, appropriate security elements must be selected to meet situation needs. *As the distributed network units become more geographically separated, decisions on which of the security elements to apply are driven lower in the organization.*

PHYSICAL PROTECTION

Physical protection is situation driven at the lowest or local level. A *general rule* may be proposed:

PREVENT UNFRIENDLY ACTS THROUGH PHYSICAL CONTACT WITH HARDWARE, LOGICAL COMPONENTS, INFORMATION, AND OPERATORS.

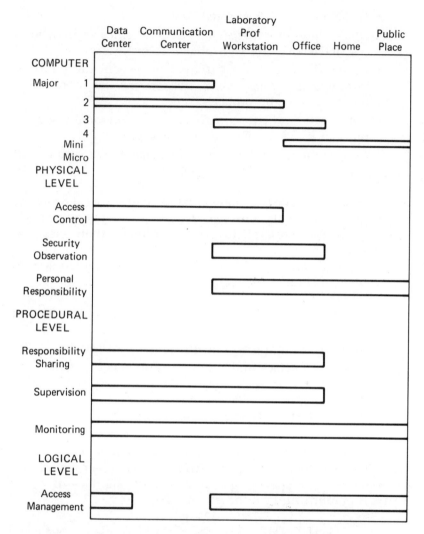

EXHIBIT 7–2. Critical Elements Across Computing Situations.

Depending on the information classification and the local environment, security elements applied from the physical level might include:

- *Data center.* A full range of elements including guards, electronic surveillance, restricted areas, and visitor escort.

- *Minicomputer.* Restricted area.
- *Office information system.* General office security with restricted areas for central service facilities.
- *Personal workstation.* Individual responsibility for following security procedure—lock door, and store documents and media properly.
- *Terminals and casual use devices.* Personal responsibility of users to follow established procedure.
- *Communications facilities.* Restricted area with locked doors.

Note that on-the-scene decisions must be made by local people so that physical security is consistent with business operations and provides protection suitable to the level of information classification at that location.

The tactics for physical security in the distributed system environment include

- Keeping unauthorized persons away from equipment and output.
- Keeping operating equipment under observation.
- Protecting cables and communications equipment.

PROCEDURAL PROTECTION

The procedural/organizational protection level includes all those work elements that make up the structure of a job or task. Properly conceived, good job design can contribute significantly to security. A *general rule* can be proposed:

LIMIT DAMAGE ANY ONE PERSON CAN DO.

Procedural security elements include

- *Personal responsibility.* The accepted awareness of, motivation to use, and compliance with procedures by individual employees. In an unstructured situation, such as use of a professional workstation, the employee must use common sense in handling situations not covered by established practices. Motivation and competence in security matters is an essential in such circumstances.

- *Job structure.* Where potential for fraud or theft exists, the job procedure should have built-in controls. Examples are supervisory reviews, audits, routine approvals, separation of duties, and double entry systems.
- *Inter- and intrasystem checks.* Where automatic or manual examination at checkpoints is needed to ensure integrity of information in process, computers provide this.
- *Security administration.* Following the established "need to know" principle, limit individual information access to that authorized and required by virtue of job assignments. This is a significant task and may include:

  — Creation of authorized user profiles to include authentication data (e.g., password) and employee information on job assignment, organization, location, etc.

  — Support of authorization procedures by which appropriate, specified levels of management can grant, deny, or cancel individual access authorizations.

  In essence, this administration activity provides the logical security level interface with the people using the system. It also monitors system use and reports attempted or successful unauthorized accesses.

When business installs distributed systems, procedural security elements are often ignored, although in the developing computing environments they are critical.

LOGICAL PROTECTION

Logical protection includes all the technical software (program) and hardware systems that control access to, and processing among, the various parts of a computer system or network. A *general rule* may be suggested:

MAKE UNAUTHORIZED ACCESS TO INFORMATION PROHIBITIVELY EXPENSIVE (DIFFICULT) RELATIVE TO INFORMATION VALUE.

Generally, there are two types of logical security elements in the logical security level. These are

- Elements controlling information transfers and processes within the system. Usually these are elements imbedded in the operating system, and security is a byproduct of rules intended to ensure integrity and safe operation. For example, certain operating system elements make sure that data being processed do not overwrite programs in core which provide instructions. Also, some elements separate different jobs so that one authorized user cannot obtain another authorized user's data.

- Elements controlling access to computer system parts from outside, such as from terminals or other system stations. Usually referred to as "access control" or "access management" systems, these elements implement the individual user authorizations described under procedural security above.

Access control logical security elements are of interest to the manager using PWA, as they are the principal means for ensuring limited access to electronic information. Effective access management elements allow for:

- Identification of an authorized user through something the user is, knows, or has. Examples are a fingerprint reader (is), a password (knows), or a magnetic plastic card (has). Any of these tokens is appropriate for identification.

- Authentication of the identified user through a second token the user is, knows, or has. This is a check against possible theft, loss, or compromise of the identification item. The access control software recognizes the authentication signal and passes control to the authorization element.

- Authorization, usually through a reference table in the computer, provides a limiting mechanism which allows the authenticated user to see or do those things authorized by management by virtue of the user's job assignments.

To be efficient, the access control software requires certain characteristics. The situation can be compared to a door. If the door has several locking devices and is specially strengthened, it will be resistant to attack, but it may be impractical for use, as the authorized entrant must carry several keys and must remember several combinations to unlock the door. In addition, considerable expense is involved in reinforcement.

Similarly, access control systems must be flexible enough to be seen as practical in the business environment where productivity is important. The system must provide for

- Identification/authentication tokens with efficient characteristics. Some of these are password length of at least seven characters, high dependability for discrimination among users, and operation reliability.
- Relatively easy change of password or other token by users; periodic changes of passwords are essential.
- Tokens used for identification or authentication processes should be stored in the computer in encrypted or encoded form, to avoid penetration by unauthorized persons who may be able to manipulate operating systems or the surrounding processing environment in the computer.

Since electronic access to information in a distributed system can be initiated from almost any place or by using a variety of devices, access control software is the single most critical positive security element. Individual commitment is also essential, especially when devices are in private homes, but this provides only a general defense. The potential for intentional damage is significant, and an efficient logical security system is the only answer.

Since a good logical access control system presupposes authorization granted to users, "information management," or the planning and control of databases used in the business, is implied. Information management (or "data management") is a complex subject beyond our scope here, but it has these parts, among others:

- Recognition of information as an important business asset requiring management.
- Standardization of data elements (the basic building blocks of information systems).
- Data definitions which provide instructions on how data elements are to be interpreted and used.

- Processes for obtaining and updating information.
- Identification of "data owners," who may also be responsible for issuing authorizations to access.

Logical security is provided by systems designers and service providers (as in the case of central data centers). Procedural security elements, which grow in importance as physical security elements become relatively inappropriate, are the responsibility of general management. The professional security staff and the organizational security manager and coordinators are the resource for development and implementation of these procedural security elements.

Security administration activities for PWA systems, including minicomputers and office information systems (OIS), include important tasks from each of the three concentric levels, that is, physical, procedural, and logical security. As computing power becomes more dispersed or distributed to personal levels and locations, the optimum mix of security elements from the levels changes. Exhibit 7–3 shows how logical elements become more important and physical protection becomes less important. This is evidence of the fact that protection of physical entities becomes extremely difficult once computer access devices are placed in private homes or public places, such as telephone booths.

Exhibit 7–4 provides an overview of the security element assignments, from the three concentric levels, for various situations. The table illustrates the variety of security applications suitable for the distributed processing environments. The secu-

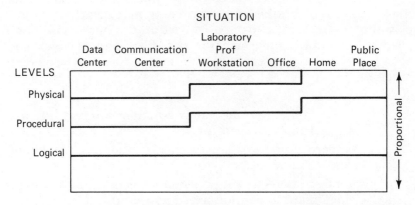

EXHIBIT 7–3. Optimal Mix of Elements from Concentric Levels.

EXHIBIT 7–4
Applying Levels of Protection When Using Minicomputers

	Configuration		Concentric Levels			
	Networked	Stand-Alone	Physical	Org. & Procedural	Logical	Data Transform
Process (manufac-turing)	X		X	X		per classifi-cation
		X	X			
Laboratory (research)	X		X		X	
		X	X			
Office system (single application)	X		X		X	
		X	X			
Professional Workstation	X		X	X	X	
		X	X			
Personal (at work or home)	X		X	X		
		X	X			

EXHIBIT 7–5
The Security Manager/Coordinator's Responsibilities in Implementing Distributed Systems (PWA)

	Elements from Concentric Levels of Security			
System Type	Physical	Procedural	Logical	Transformational (registered data only)
Minicomputer				
Stand-alone	R	C	A	A
Networked	R	C	A	A
Professional				
workstation	C	A	A	A
Systems devices and network	R	C	A	A
Terminal	C	C	A	A
Word processor	C	C	A	A
Personal				
minicomputer	A	A	A	A
Facsimile	R	C	A	A
Communications facility	R	C	n/a	n/a

R—Responsible for implementing protection.
C—Consultive—participates in definition of elements.
A—Advisory only—systems designers or technicians have responsibility.

rity elements from the three levels are not only adaptable to varying circumstances but can also be selected from among the many alternatives to meet business requirements as to cost, placement, monitoring, practicality, etc. This flexibility is an important reason why the security manager should understand the concept of the three levels and their contents, the many security elements.

The business manager must be concerned about the use of distributed computing, whether through personal workstation automation or minicomputers. The important areas for security are those which concern the procedural aspects of distributed computing.

The task of ensuring the security of business information processed on computing systems has many parts. Some significant parts are well within the capability of the informed and motivated security coordinator or manager. Those parts have been described and are illustrated in Exhibit 7–5.

8

Personal Workstation Automation Security Vulnerabilities

In *The Shockwave Rider,* J. Brunner developed the notion of an omnipotent "tapeworm" program running loose through a network of computers—an idea which may seem rather disturbing, but which is also quite beyond our current capabilities. The basic model, however, remains a very provocative one: a program or a computation that can move from machine to machine, harnessing resources as needed, and replicating itself when necessary. . . .

In recent years, it has become possible to pursue these ideas in newly emerging, richer computing environments: large numbers of powerful computers, connected with a local computer network and a full architecture of internetwork protocols, and supported by a diverse set of specialized network servers. Against this background, we have undertaken the development and operation of several real, multimachine "worm" programs. . . .

John F. Shoch and Jon A. Hupp[17]

Since information is an important asset of any competitive business, any change in the way we handle information must be considered against the current background of increasing industrial espionage, fast-developing technology, and economic attack, both inter- and intranational. We have seen that personal workstation automation involves some spectacular changes in the way we will handle information in the course of operating a business. We must identify the security vulnerabilities resulting from the new information-handling and processing applications that we have called PWA.

Many of the security vulnerabilities noted in office or professional PWA systems uses are the same as those found in the traditional office. Where a business management has been aware of information security needs and has provided for the protection of valuable information, some significant adjustments may be required. For those who are only now becoming aware of the vulnerabilities of competitive information, the arrival of PWA systems should add a sense of urgency to their recognition of the need for an information security program. One would like to avoid a tired rehash of the need for protecting documents and avoiding loose talk. Let it be noted that these traditional security rules continue to be important.

We have seen that electronic information systems, and especially distributed systems as represented by PWA, change the spatial and time constraints associated with information in paper forms. We will see that these changes cause a number of new security vulnerabilities to occur.

PWA RISK ENVIRONMENTS

Three different risk environments can be suggested where PWA systems are in use. This arrangement is merely one selected for convenience by the author; security managers who have studied their company's applications of PWA may come up with several more. The three risk environments are

1. Controlled-risk environment, such as an office, laboratory, or engineering section where the business managers have positive control, to whatever extent desired, over the access to, and activities in, the facility.
2. Public high-risk environment, where company managers have little or no control over access or activities.

3. Home medium-risk environment, where, although we must assume a minimum level of loyalty from employees, events may be uncontrollable or may lead to improper activities.

Exhibit 8–1 shows exemplary sets of PWA systems in various risk environments. The letters in circles illustrate particular information security vulnerabilities that may occur in the risk environment indicated.

From a security viewpoint, we have *two distinct communications environments.* First, for intralocation message traffic (including facsimile and voice), we have a local network completely under our control, assuming proper installation. Second, for interlocation traffic, we have a serious exposure as our messages travel across lines and through switching centers controlled by others.

Communications remaining within our building or campus can be restrained to devices, communications controllers, and wires to which the security manager can apply physical and, if appropriate, procedural security measures. Logical security elements (e.g., passwords) can protect against unauthorized access to messsages from connections with the public networks.

Generally, the following are minimal requirements for protecting PWA networks internal to a business building or campus.

- Communications cables should be in a conduit or trench whenever the cables are outside of directly controlled areas. For example, if a business shares a facility with others, and cables must pass through areas that are public or controlled by others, the cable should be shielded.
- Devices that provide central file storage for a network and units that control communications functions should be secured in "restricted areas," where only specially authorized employees can enter.

When local networks connect through "gateways" to public utility networks, protection of information is beyond the immediate control of the security manager. However, users should be made aware that a lesser degree of security applies when a message passes to the public networks.

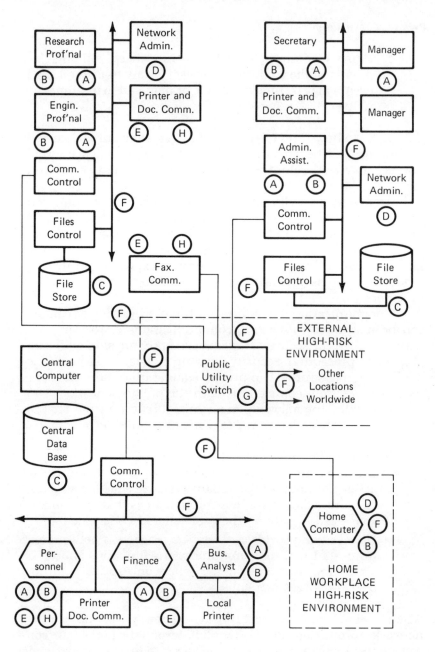

EXHIBIT 8–1. Personal Workstation Automation and Security Vulnerability.

KEY

Management
Workstation

Personal
Computer

Professional
Workstation

Document
Processors

Coaxial Cable

Security Vulnerabilities

A   VDT display to unauthorized persons
B   Media theft
C   Unauthorized data modification, change, destruction
D   Unauthorized access due to administrative control failure
E   Document theft or unauthorized observation
F   Unauthorized connections or taps
G   Communications observation by unauthorized parties
H   Unauthorized transmission

Public Systems

The most severe risks from the use of PWA systems have to do with this uncontrolled or "public" environment. In the traditional business information process, this type of risk became a concern only when employees carried documents off business premises, carried on telephone conversations concerning sensitive matters, or sent telegrams containing valuable or potentially embarrassing information. With PWA systems, the communications network capabilities greatly increase this vulnerability. A networked PWA system (remember that a large part of the value of PWA is in communications) almost always will use public utility services to connect remote buildings or campuses. This is because of the investment necessary to replace existing wire and radio (satellite?) communications connections. Once the business information message or document (in electronic form) leaves the controlled business premises, we are faced with some fairly severe risks. Among those are

- Improper actions by employees of the servicing communications carrier, who may observe, copy, or change messages, or divert them to unauthorized stations.
- Systems failures in the utility switching computers, which could misroute, garble, or destroy information.
- Wire tapping or radio message interception, which could allow copying of all traffic with the subsequent luxury for the interceptor of a casual analysis and selection of interesting items. Increasing use of radio transmissions must be highly suspect from an information security view. Interception of radio transmissions is now a major activity for government intelligence, and there is little reason to assume that business intelligence will be far behind. Recent events concerning technical document theft will increase interest in the less risky alternative of electronic spying.
- Unauthorized entry to the PWA network through clandestine connections to wires, which might be simple taps to telephone networks or to high-speed coaxial cable, which would allow the miscreant to use an intelligent terminal device and to actually perform processing, manipulate files, or insert programs.

The answer to these high-risk external environment exposures lies in encryption of information, typically through a computer hardware device that uses a secret key to "scramble" information to make it unintelligible to outsiders. Other logical
security systems protect information (according to its value)
through creating a series of passwords or other means for identifying and authenticating an authorized user and then limiting
what that user may do once connected to the system. Remember
that PWA systems will often give access to our large databases in
central computer centers. (Logical security elements are dicussed
in detail in the following chapter.)

Home Computing

A novel risk situation is developing in the use of home computing.
Some businesses have tested cottage industry home work situations, principally because that arrangement saves considerable
investment in facilities. In the usual case, a professional is given a
communicating workstation at home, and he or she performs all
tasks there, coming to the business office only for meetings. We
will also be seeing increasing "take home" work, using computers, terminals, or other PWA systems, by executives and professionals. As we have noted earlier, PWA allows instant communications with files, making the primary reason for having an
"office"—access to files—less attractive. PWA will also allow the
home worker to leave messages for people at the office or at any
other station worldwide. Such systems are already in use in rudimentary form by many businesses.

The home environment is not always risk free. Family members and friends may find that using the PWA system is fun or has
potential for doing things that the business manager would find
worrisome. At a minimum, unauthorized use of business
computing resources could clog up communications lines and
bring about demand for computer capacity not justified for business reasons. In a worst case scenario, persons originally using
the home PWA system for entertainment or experimentation may
discover opportunities for damage or fraud. In a period when job
stability is questionable, such a vulnerability must be given serious consideration.

Protection against the risks in the home working environment must be based on the "need to know" principle. In other

words, we must use logical access control systems which: (1) identify and authenticate users, wherever located, and (2) positively limit what users may see and do via those data and actions required for the assigned tasks. The manager must recognize, however, that there is an increasing population of computer "hackers" (experts who enjoy experimenting with security systems) who, if given sufficient time at a connected PWA system, will eventually break through the access control software. One fairly sure protection against this kind of attempt is good administration of the logical access control keys or passwords. Frequently changed passwords and an authorization list that is kept current make the penetrator's task much more difficult.

The home PWA system is an excellent example of the severe risks involved in allowing universal access—where anyone who can "sign on" then has capability to do anything within his or her capabilities from a technical viewpoint. Limitation of what users can do, once identified and authenticated, is most important to control potential damage from parties unknown.

Of course, we are concerned about potential loss of magnetic media, such as disks, and paper outputs in the home environment. More than once, critical business strategy papers have shown up on the back of neighborhood projects or children's drawings.

Controlled Systems

Within business-controlled environments, such as offices, plants, engineering areas, and laboratories, PWA presents only a medium risk from physical information exposure. Logical or electronic exposures are another matter. Most cases of industrial espionage or damage to information from carelessness, stupidity, or intentional malicious actions are caused by employees. Most of the time, these employees are people who have authorized access to the information damaged, stolen, or used to commit fraud. Exhibit 8–2 shows types of computer-related crimes at banks and insurance companies.

It is important that PWA systems be designed to control who can access and what users can do when identified and authenticated. Limitation of employee actions, especially against central files and programs, is based on cleverly designed control mechanisms and effective administration of system activities. The tradi-

EXHIBIT 8–2[11]
Cases of Computer-Related Fraud

Methodology	Number of Cases	
	Banking	Insurance
Introduction, creation, or authorization of improper or unauthorized input	43.	30
Manipulation of input during data entry	30	2
Manipulation of computer processing	1	—
Manipulation of rejects	2	—
Diversion of output	1	—
Manipulation of data files	4	1
Manipulation or development of programs for improper use	3	—
Manipulation of hardware and systems software	—	—
Improper or unauthorized access to information or inquiry	1	1
Total	85	34

tional checks and balances, separation of duties, and good audit trails are even more important. The use of PWA systems may make auditing more difficult, as the "paper trails" and signature approvals may be less evident. Carefully designed systems will continue to provide administrative and procedural controls, allowing for follow-up and investigations of unexplained or questionable activities in PWA and connected computer systems.

While we are on the subject of controls, it is worthwhile to note that, in developing traditional information processing systems, management has an opportunity to ensure that suitable intersystem controls are in place. These will see to it that data transferred among systems are consistently defined. This is most critical when management decisions are based on information outputs. Also, most large system developments use COBOL or another business programming language that provides documentation of what the system does.

In using PWA systems, we must be extremely cautious. The very power of these systems may expose business information through inept use of information retrieval methods by individual users. Consider the situation where a development engineer wishes to assemble a file of the comments and suggestions of colleagues on alternatives for a new product. The engineer sends PWA system messages to a dozen or so people connected at distant locations and receives replies that are stored in the PWA central files at his office building. Assume that the engineer does nothing to protect the messages or files. We have serious exposures:

- Both messages and files could possibly be obtained by any person connected to the network within the company, merely by browsing through the file subject listing, using any PWA access device keyboard and screen. Printed copies of anything of interest could be made.
- Persons outside the company, who have access to interconnecting networks, have good potential for gaining this information. Remember that, as soon as a network connects with a public utility system, everyone on that utility becomes a potential "information trespasser."
- As soon as the original messages and replies leave the local internal network and enter the public utility system, the messages are subject to eavesdropping and copying at any of the utility's switching centers, by wiretapping at any location where the signal travels by wire, or by signal interception where radio transmission is used.

This situation not only reinforces the need for a wide personal awareness of and responsibility for information security, but it also points out special vulnerabilities for businesses whose technology may be competitive to that of the public utility itself. In such cases, encryption of traffic going by way of public networks is most desirable, as it provides the only reliable security assurance. Files must be adequately protected by access control systems (Chapter 10).

Managers should be aware that a general proliferation and unplanned distribution of information via PWA is not desirable. We must work with the business *information manager* (or system manager) to ensure proper control.

Managers must be aware also of the open-ended nature of the capabilities of PWA systems. Because the functions and utilities (e.g., document storage device) of the automated workstation are often not visible, or at best merely represented by an indicator or "icon" on the display, events may take place which are not purposefully planned. For example, consider the system operator, perhaps using a communicating word processor or an intelligent copier, who inadvertently transposes the address characters for a broadcast distribution (one in which a pre-established set of people are to be sent a message or memo). This error would result in the memo or message being sent to the wrong group of people. Note that no signal or warning occurs, and the sender does not have the opportunity afforded by the envelope-stuffing process to notice a pending error. Cases of this sort have already caused consternation and embarrassment. More serious results might be anticipated if the message concerned financial or competitive data that could be harmful or illegal.

Of course, single-address messsages can also be missent, but this is less likely because most of us have regular correspondents and will be well aware of their address codes.

Employees using PWA systems may develop (program) applications that also produce management decision information. But integration between applications may be extremely difficult, and consistency may be lost. The people developing PWA application will not necessarily be bound by the established system standards in the company. A loss of control or opportunity for fraud through generation of misleading or falsified data may occur. Chris Edwards, MA, ACMA, says, "One aspect of greatest importance is the need to understand the need for and methods of incorporating internal security systems into the process of creating micro-based (i.e., personal workstation) systems. The problems resulting from lack of security discovered in the early 1960s when developing mainframe systems need not be repeated; the understanding is available; it only needs to be passed on to the developers of microcomputer-based systems."[13]

Suitably secure cabinets must be provided for the storage of magnetic media and documents. A major task seems to be involved in getting those who use PWA systems to think of magnetic media as being the same as paper in terms of information value. In several noted cases (see Chapter 9), tapes and disks have been lost because they were not secured in the same way as the output documents. Other vulnerabilities in the business environment include casual observation of information on VDTs (display screens), incorrect distribution of messages or documents through PWA electronic message systems or facsimile systems (especially broadcast or multiple-addressee type distributions), and browsing through electronic files using an authorized PWA unit or an unauthorized unit that had been carelessly left in a "signed-on" status.

EMBEDDED PASSWORDS

Many of the microcomputers found in personal workstation automation systems will be used in conjunction with microcomputer
communications devices. (The so-called "smart" modems used to
connect a PWA system to a telephone line enable the user to write
short programs to make the communications connection.) Most
people will quickly recognize the opportunity to make life easier
by creating a macro instruction set, one which will perform a
number of instructions on command.

Within the macro will be the central computer telephone
number, the instruction codes for the modem or microcomputer
telephone connector, and the user's password. Thus, once the
user has mounted his systems disk or has read in the tape containing the access macro program, all that is needed is a program
"call." That is, the user keys into his or her keyboard the name of
the macro program. The PWA computer then performs the functions of awakening the modem, dialing the central computer's
number, getting the data carrier tone, and making the prelimi-
nary connection by entering the account codes and the password.
The entire logical security procedure is now embedded in the access macro program. All that is needed to access this user account
is to know the macro program call name, which is probably available in the PWA system's file index.

Careful protection of the systems disk now becomes para-
mount. The efficiency of the computer itself has threatened to
negate the carefully contrived protection system. Security in such
a case depends totally on the motivation of the PWA user to apply
proper procedure in locking up the systems disk when the user is
not present. Leaving the system run with the disk mounted is
tantamount to leaving the account "signed on," since the logical
access identification and authentication elements are stored as
part of the macro program.

INFORMATION CHANGE OF FORM

A special security vulnerability occurs when information changes
form. Consider the situation where an order entry clerk is reading
customer orders received by mail and entering the data via a personal workstation, to be transmitted later to a central computer
where order processing and customer billing are done. At one

place, the clerk has the original customer order and an electronic representation of the order on the VDT screen. There is potential for fraud because there is no positive match between the information forms. The clerk could change the order in terms of merchandise, credit, delivery instructions, customer, etc. In fact, this particular stage in the use of PWA systems is where most fraud or computer systems misuse occurs.

In other situations, where information exists in more than one form at one place, the opportunity to substitute documents, make improper entries to a PWA system, remove or steal documents, or change critical data makes fraud attractive. In one of the cases described later in this book, a clerk makes delivery entries to allow friends to pick up materials that are not properly accounted for; the paper forms at the workstation either are destroyed or never existed.

Managers must recognize that audit trails, which were easily constructed and manually checked in old paper-based systems, may no longer be possible in PWA computerized methods. Where a supervisor or a worker at a subsequent process could check an entry for accuracy and validity, the personal workstation now enters the data directly into the computer, where all the various processes take place. Although the computer system (which may be built into the workstation in some cases) may be able to check among various files for consistency and may perform validation routines, discrepancies caused through improper entries or paper handling may not be traceable.

Often, when information processes are converted to computer system operations, the checks and balances that may have been natural to the manual system are overlooked or are not provided for. As most managers know, fraud requires collusion, and frequently, the automated system offers the chance to commit fraud with fewer parties involved. One person inside the system operation and one person outside—perhaps in a customer's office—may be all that is needed to perpetrate a continuing theft of goods or services because the automated system will often assume that the generation of questionable charges or shipments will be a trigger to alert management. The "outside" person, of course, destroys or hides these evidential invoices, tickets, or other systems-generated documents.

In the design of a PWA system, then, particular attention must be paid to those circumstances where critical data exist in more than one form. Almost all PWA systems have information in at least two forms, but careful consideration should reveal those workstations where high risk exists. Documents that establish fiscal responsibility or which have financial implications should be carefully controlled through batching or numbering. When input documents are to be thrown away after use, the destruction of the papers should be controlled if a potential for misuse is evident. Finally, where PWA systems are used as inputs to other processes, such as order entry, manual audit points should be established at subsequent steps to allow management to ensure accurate, complete data.

9

Cases of Fraud and Deception Using PWA

We are fast approaching the time when one out of every ten people in the work force will have a direct working relationship with computers. With the number of installed computers approaching the half-million mark and proliferating more rapidly as a result of minicomputers and microprocessors, there is not much doubt that computer fraud will grow proportionately.

Leonard Krauss and Eileen MacGahan[24]

The use of cases to explain theory is traditional, and for security purposes, it is unusually effective. This is so because everything we do is based upon a chance happening—that the crisis or attack for which we have prepared will actually occur. When we see or hear about security problems that have actually occurred, it clarifies our thinking. We do not want to make the mistake of the generals and "prepare for the last war."

The cases described here actually occurred, but all the details have been changed to protect the privacy of those involved. All of these circumstances were reported in the press or were provided to the author by professional acquaintances. Any direct identifications or situational similarities are coincidental.

THE MISCHIEF CLUB

Brain Corporation is involved with the development of industrial robots and other sophisticated electronic industrial equipment. Brain uses many computers and has a number of internal networks that connect central computer centers with minicomputers and terminals in offices and laboratories. Many of these devices are personal workstation automation (PWA) systems.

Brain's scientists and engineers had been reporting systems problems in using their PWA devices, such as loss of files and communications interference. When unauthorized files appeared in a central database, Brain's security began an investigation. Partially through information provided by an informant, and through data gathered from system monitor records (which recorded computer use histories), it became apparent that an organized attempt was being made to disrupt Brain's business operations.

Eventually, through network connections to the general research and university communities, an informal "club" of university people and computer hobbyists was uncovered. Because of the very extensive communications provided by the Brain networks, which reached outside the company into many related technical communities, really tight security on access to the network was not practical, so Brain was vulnerable to damage by groups like the club.

The club operated in the following manner. Members exchanged a letter, often by means of the network itself, which provided actual or assumed information on passwords, access methods, types of computers contacted, and so forth. Members would then play with this information, using personal terminals, developing ever more complete access data that eventually allowed ready entry to Brain Corporation's computer systems. Once connected, some members merely experimented to see what they could do. Some actually performed computing tasks—in effect, stealing computer services from Brain. A few people tried to do mischief by destroying files or by entering programs that would confuse systems users. In some cases, minors were used to do the actual damage—thus making successful prosecution more unlikely.

Analysis

This type of sabotage to a PWA system is extremely difficult to prevent. Damage can be controlled, however, through effective password management, where user passwords are frequently changed in line with information values and threat levels. At Brain Corporation more frequent changes of access control passwords would have frustrated the purpose of the club newsletter and made progressive development of access information impossible, or at least much more difficult.

The importance of: (1) monitoring systems activities, and (2) administering access control systems cannot be overstated. Logical security elements are usually fairly effective, but when the externals, such as review of systems problems logs, or reminders to have (or force) users to change passwords are disregarded, we enter a high-risk situation. Brain had basic security elements in place, but a relaxed atmosphere allowed outsiders to play with the systems until a dangerous situation had developed.

CARRY-OUT SERVICE

Consulting Engineering (CE), Ltd., performed construction, design, and management tasks on contract. Customer contracts were written by CE's operating and legal staffs using PWA devices, and the results were automatically fed to word processing systems, where the contracts were polished and put into final form. The contracts were then printed out and sent to legal officers for final review before signing by company officers and customers.

The final contract documents were handled as "private" information and were locked in a safe when not in use. The electronic, or digital, forms of the contracts were kept on magnetic disks produced by the PWA system. The typists had a carousel-type file that was set on a filing cabinet, and the disks were put in this file, which allowed efficient access for the many changes and references required in daily contract development work.

On arriving for work one morning, the typists found the entire carousel file missing. It was never recovered. Consulting Engineering, Ltd.'s, pricing strategy and contracts file had been exposed.

Analysis

People tend to forget that information is information, no matter what form it is in. Consulting Engineering took pains to secure its documents but completely failed to recognize that the same critical private information was present in the little disks stored so casually on a filing cabinet. Security requires that we think in terms of systems wherever PWA systems are in use. Traditional physical forms protection just won't do.

HELP YOURSELF

The warehouse at Paper Products, Inc., contained tons of finished paper products, such as paper plates, tablecloths, party supplies, and decorative items. Orders from dealers were received by telephone by six clerks, who used computer terminals to effect a complete order cycle. The clerks received calls based on the geographic area in which the customer was located. Upon receiving a call, the clerk made certain that the customer was within the assigned area and then checked the customer's account credit status. If the customer had not established credit, the call was transferred to the credit department, where a manager used a terminal to set up appropriate arrangements. If the customer had credit available, the clerk entered the order. The computer system then printed out a shipping ticket, debited the customer's account, and deducted the items shipped from inventory. The clerk could indicate if an order was to be picked up at the warehouse and could also indicate "ship to other" or "bill to other."

As set up, the system did not separate accounts by area. That separation was done only by the incoming-telephone-call controller. This meant that any one of the six clerks taking orders could look at accounts belonging to the other five clerks. Also, the system did not provide for identification and authentication of the clerks when the terminals were turned on for use. As it happened, some customers began complaining about being billed for shipments or items not received. Investigation showed that unidentified parties were creating bogus pick-up orders with a "bill to other" indication. Since there was no way to track system entries to a specific terminal, management could not ascertain who had made these entries.

Analysis

Any personal workstation automation system should provide an audit trail that positively identifies system users if a potential for fraud exists. Also, a PWA system that allows access to a central database, as in this instance, must limit authorized accessors to that information needed to do the job. Each clerk should have been limited to the set of accounts assigned to the geographic area that he or she serviced, and no others. Paper-based audit trails used in traditional systems were effective because the papers themselves left clues, such as handwriting, and allowed simple checking of actions by a supervisor. Electronic systems involving PWA may not offer such opportunity for control; unless the system is carefully constructed with security and auditability in mind, opportunity for fraud or mischief may be attractive to some employees.

COMPUTER CAPER

Processing Machines Corporation built electronic systems. A network of personal workstation automation systems in and among the plants of Processing Machines provided a communications system used for administrative and technical message traffic. Information stored in individual files was protected, but information sent over the network as messages could be collected by network users who cared to inquire, through terminals, into the system's disk files.

One user was able to collect enough information to build up a complete history of the problems surrounding a controversial product, although this employee was not privy to the information through normal organizational channels.

Analysis

Any use of a networked PWA system must be considered to have serious security complications. Distribution of information by electronic systems changes the time and spatial constraints typical of paper-based information distributions. Unless specific security elements are applied, one cannot assume that information sent to another is private to the two parties involved. Continual use of PWA systems by skilled individuals often turns up weaknesses in system controls that allow unauthorized observation or modification of information.

YOU CAN'T TAKE IT WITH YOU

A vendor-supplied network and computer service was used by Auto Transfer Company, a shipper of automobiles, for communicating delivery schedules, delivery of automobiles, vehicle availabilities, receipting, and general company correspondence. Also, the company performed various computing tasks using the vendor's computing services. Access was through a series of interconnected personal workstations. The vendor provided effective access controls and information security controls through client-operated file naming and password services.

Auto Transfer discovered that the vendor was billing for services which could not be identified. Investigation showed that certain vendor employees, who had been in positions of trust and had access to Auto Transfer's passwords and file names, had been using Auto Transfer's files as a basis for computer processing. Although in a distant city, these ex-employees of the computer service vendor were able to access the vendor's computer using Auto Transfer's codes. In essence, these people were stealing computing services from the vendor and charging the costs to Auto Transfer. In the process, they also had *carte blanche* access to Auto Transfer's files.

Analysis

Auto Transfer had failed to use the password control system in an effective manner by neglecting to periodically change the passwords. The miscreants, having surreptitiously obtained the passwords through their privileged positions at the vendor, were able to use those passwords over a period of time. Had Auto Transfer changed the passwords, as per good security practice, the exposure of their business information could not have occurred. Whenever PWA systems use files which are, or could be, shared, proper logical (i. e., through software) and procedural security elements are an absolute requirement.

LOOK WHAT WE'VE GOT

When Benjamin Company's computer operator started up the computer system on Monday morning, he was astounded to see a payroll listing printing out. It was not a format he had seen before, and he had no jobs running on his computer. He called his supervisor, and before long, the listing had found its way to Benjamin's vice president. It was evident to the v.p. that this was an executive payroll listing from a company hundreds of miles distant from Benjamin's city. A few telephone calls located the owner of the listing. Benjamin company returned the payroll listing by mail that same day.

Analysis

Luckily, the exposure of this sensitive document was limited by the integrity of the people at Benjamin Company who came in contact with it. An investigation by the owner of the payroll listing showed that Benjamin shared a network with that business. In the course of normal operations, a processing device had developed mechanical trouble. The payroll printing file was held in the system during a period when software changes were being made. A combination of circumstances impossible to foresee had resulted in the payroll data's being transmitted to the distant terminal, instead of one located near the originating computer.

The people involved in the immediate situation had failed to notify data processing of the actual status of the report after the device failed. Thus, one group believed the listing had completed printing; the other believed the matter was being "handled." The listing obviously had ideas of its own and ended up at Benjamin's terminal. Good security awareness and the motivation to exercise due care could have avoided this incident, a not uncommon occurrence in these days of multiple network interconnects.

10

Designing Personal Workstation Automation for Secure Operation

---

As computers emerge from their years of infancy, they are taking on increasingly responsible work. We do not know how far this process will go or how responsible the computer will eventually become in society. We can only observe its prodigious growth in capability and potential. The more vital the work of the computer becomes, the more important it is to protect it from failure and catastrophe and from criminals, vandals, incompetents, and people who would misuse its power.

James Martin[23]

Systems design is generally considered foreign to the average business manager's set of skills. With the impending widespread use of personal workstation automation, the manager's best opportunity to effect good security is during the system design activity. Once the PWA system is in place and being used, security problems may be very difficult to resolve. The manager then must understand the process used to develop personal workstation automation systems applications so that he or she may address intelligently the placement of security decisions within this process.

The design of a PWA system may vary quite a bit from company to company or among situations. However, the process outlined here is fairly common and is one which a leading com-

EXHIBIT 10–1

The Security Manager's Responsibilities in Implementing PWA Systems

	Elements from Concentric Levels of Security			
System Type	*Physical*	*Procedural*	*Logical*	*Transformational*
Minicomputer				
Stand-alone	R	C	A	A
Networked	R	C	A	A
Professional				
workstation (8000)	C	A	A	A
Systems devices				
and network	R	C	A	A
Terminal	C	C	A	A
Word processor	C	C	A	A
Personal				
minicomputer	A	A	A	A
Facsimile	R	C	A	A
Communications facility	R	C	n/a	n/a

R—Responsible for implementing protection.
C—Consultive—participates in definition of elements.
A—Advisory only—systems designers or technicians have responsibility.

pany in the field finds effective. One thing is certain—if your company is just installing equipment without the more formal studies suggested here, you are missing an opportunity to enjoy the productivity benefits available from PWA. Exhibit 10–1 suggests security roles in the development and installation process.

The process suggested has six discrete activities. Security does not have a part to play in every activity, but we should be familiar with the flow of this process so that proper security inputs may be ensured.

PWA ANALYSIS AND SYSTEMS DESIGN PROCESS

Activity 1   PWA Study Introduction and Outline

The persons assigned responsibility for designing and installing the personal workstation automation system must hold communications meetings with the managers and employees in the business functions or work areas to be affected. During these meetings the analysts become familiar with the people and the organization. A general project approach is developed, based on this process. The appropriate SECURITY elements subjects should appear in the tentative project outline proposed at this stage.

Activity 2 Organization and Work Study

The analysts must be absolutely certain that the organizational functions and missions are understood. To this end, a top-down overview of the organization is needed, including definitions of objectives. Interviews with the people involved are the basis for the overview. All managers and a sampling of the staff should be included. Among the data to be generated are: (1) critical success factors, (2) means for measurement of success of the functions to apply PWA, and (3) the information needs of the function. In this activity, the manager must ensure that INFORMATION VALUES (classifications) are established. During this activity, it may become evident to the analysts that methods improvements can be suggested. This is critical, as effective methods and information flows are crucial to PWA success. In other words, do not automate a function that has poorly designed processes.

Activity 3 Workstation Analysis

A detailed analysis at the working level (microanalysis) in this activity will be done based on time and activity logs. These logs are prepared by the managers and professionals who are projected for PWA applications. The detailed data generated will allow a projection of productivity benefits. For example, if electronic document transfer is involved in the projected system, this activity may show considerable savings from elimination of delays in document reviews. SECURITY content in this activity may include any special physical or logical processes required to protect high-value information.

Activity 4 PWA System Definition

The actual selection of hardware and software PWA system components takes place during this stage. SECURITY elements from the physical and logical levels (e.g., locking equipment, media storage equipment, information access control programs, system monitoring programs) must be specified during this activity. Such decisions are based on the information valuation established in Activity 2. Also, SECURITY procedural aspects must be defined; in other words, how will PWA system managers control the granting and denial of access to the information processed or stored in the PWA system? Recall our earlier discussion in Chapters 5 and 6 about the importance of effective administration.

Activity 5   PWA Recommendation

In this activity, the analysts finalize their recommendations and present them to responsible management and to the people involved, following the organization's usual practices for approvals. We should participate in these recommendations to make certain that the using managers understand the reasoning behind the SECURITY requirements and to gain acceptance and support among the prospective PWA system operators.

Activity 6   Operational Analysis

Once installed and in use, PWA system operations must be measured and analyzed to demonstrate benefits from the investment. Among the items to be measured is SECURITY. Is the set of security elements provided achieving the protection required for the information values established?

Responsible managers can no longer afford to sit on the sidelines while important decisions are made that may directly affect the security of an important business asset, namely information. To participate in the decision process, the manager must understand personal workstation automation concepts and must establish a role in the process of defining PWA system and supporting administrative activities. Exhibit 10–2 shows the flow of activity and the security manager's role.

DEALING WITH COMPUTER SPECIALISTS

There is often a problem, or at least people perceive it as one, in dealing with technical specialists. They seem to speak in strange tongues and have goals and reasons that may appear out of touch

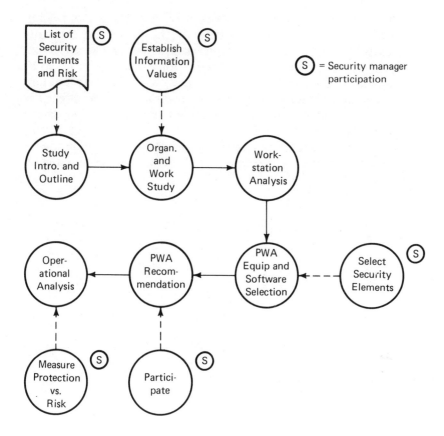

EXHIBIT 10–2. Personal Workstation Automation Analysis and Design Process.

with the layman's vision of the business situation. A most helpful angle on the problem, when security is discussed, is that most computer technologists already have a keen sense of the vulnerabilities of personal workstation automation and hence an understanding of the need for protection.

The office/lab/plant manager who wants to get the technologists involved in designing or implementing proper security in PWA systems must first convince the computer specialist that he or she understands the problem. This is not an understanding of the technical systems—the hardware and software—but rather an understanding of what the PWA system is and does. We have explained in detail the optimum role of the security manager in the design process, which by its nature requires a technician. The system designer is an expert in the technical elements constituting the PWA system; the security manager is an expert in the protection requirements needed for the information to be processed. Both expert views are needed to do an adequate job.

To some degree, the average manager's ability to affect the outcome will depend on his or her role per management definition. An ability to explain information values convincingly is also important. The primary purpose of this book is to provide the security manager or business manager with the knowledge necessary to do so.

11

A Primer for Protecting Information in Personal Workstation Automation Systems

---

When a manager participates in the PWA system selection process, he or she must know about the elements required to achieve an acceptable level of information security. This primer is intended to provide such knowledge. The primer begins with definitions of applicable terms and proceeds with a discussion of the use of the PWA security elements.

DEFINITIONS

Secure PWA System: A system or unit which

1. Maintains the reliability and integrity of the information processed; in other words, this system is reliable to a degree which allows the user to assume that data entered will later be found to be complete as entered and free from damage or improper modification.

2. Permits the system user to specify the access authorizations he or she desires, according to varying levels of information sensitivity or value (classification), and by individual user, according to authorizations for access and manipula-

tion, conveniently and without extensive administrative difficulty.

3. Establishes a penetration work factor that is commensurate with the information values assigned.

4. Maintains records of system accesses to valuable information to allow security managers to audit system activity.

Penetration Work Factor: The effort and/or resources (i. e., cost) required for an unauthorized person to successfully penetrate a system and as a result, to obtain, damage, or change valuable information. Effective security results in a penetration work factor that suits the value of the information being protected. As an example, if a file has an assumed value of one million dollars, security measures should cause the penetrator to spend at least that much to obtain the data. Obviously, in real life, we do not have such crisp definition, but the reasoning is valid.

Security Elements: The security measures that fall within categories set up according to the basic characteristics of the measures. For example, security elements may be physical, procedural, and/or logical (includes transformation or encryption).

DISCUSSION

Personal workstation automation systems that will be used to process, store, or communicate valuable business information should contain a combination of security elements. The particular combination of elements depends on the circumstances of system use. In every case, the set of security elements selected must establish a penetration work factor suitable to the value or classification of the information processed. Security elements are often interchangeable, allowing system designers to provide a combination of protections tailored to the circumstances. As an example, a locked, secure room could be an alternative to a password access control used on a PWA system situated in an open area. The manager must consider the situation and work with the system designer to achieve security appropriate to the system use and information values.

Unless the PWA system offers some inherent information security capabilities, achieving appropriate security can be a difficult task. That is why it is important for the security manager to participate in early phases of PWA system selection.

Two or more types of security elements are almost always required. Some typical security element combinations might be

- Physical, procedural, and logical
- Physical and procedural
- Logical, procedural, and transformational

Note that physical security elements, of themselves, are satisfactory only when the PWA system can stand alone (not connected to any other devices or systems) or is hard wired to a closed system. (The individual PWA connects with specific files and cannot be used for other purposes or routings to other systems.) Such cases are unusual in that logical security elements are almost always required to ensure the exclusivity of use or connections.

Valid security element combinations for PWA may be selected from among these:

- *Physical.* Strong, lockable, steel cabinets; lockable power switch; secure media storage cabinets; display privacy screens; controlled access rooms.
- *Procedural.* Records of authorized system users and what they are permitted to do; for example, each may have varying authorization to see information, change information (modify), delete information, or run programs. Lists for physical access control. Processing of employee job and authorization changes. Monitoring of system access records. Monitoring of employee password maintenance. (A password that is not changed becomes a public password.)
- *Logical.* Includes software (usually programs that run with the operating system supplied by the manufacturer but may be programs that are part of an applications package). Such software may provide access control by allowing the data owner to specify: (1) user identification or use of something the user knows, is, or has, to claim a specific personal identity; (2) user authentication or proof of the identity claimed through something the user knows, is, or has; and (3) authorization to do or see a specific thing by means of a preset table or reference in the system. Security software elements also assist users in

signing on, track and limit user actions, and protect information from inadvertent or intentional damage during processing.

Effective security software elements will allow a user to define a logical information file as

- Private to the individual user, or
- Shared among a specific group, with whom the user (owner) shares certain identity characteristics, or
- Public to any user having access. With current network development, this could be almost anyone.

The access that each user has in such a case is determined by the system's matching the authentication element against a preset table of authorizations.

Logical security measures include encryption or encipherment of information through the use of a mathematical algorithm. Encrypted information is represented by a nonrepeating random substitution of numbers and characters that is sufficiently complex to make interpretation or decryption almost impossible without a key. Encryption is the strongest information security measure available; it is also expensive and requires absolutely foolproof administration—unless the keys are managed by the system itself. If you manually handle keys and you lose one, you have lost the data. (The keys are typically very large numbers.)

A BRIEF LOOK AT TRANSFORMATION (ENCRYPTION)

Transformation of information, using codes, is as old as warfare and writing. Encryption, encipherment, and encoding all mean the use of some system to transform information so that a person without a key cannot understand the messages or data that have been coded. Since all software has faults, it is difficult to conceive of a computer system that cannot be penetrated. As we know, physical security measures can also fail or can be successfully attacked.

It is evident that, in critical cases, we cannot rely on either the logical or physical security barriers. Encryption offers a highly dependable alternative that is resistant to all but the most sophisticated attack. It is expensive, and some applications of encryption, although technically feasible and conceptually practical, have never been commercially implemented. Such is the case with the "network security control center" and automated key distribution and control. Current uses of encryption are very localized—that is, data are encrypted for transmission from one point to another or for storage on tape or disk. (This limitation excludes military situations, where cost is a secondary consideration.)

In every case, the information or message is fed into a hardware device or processed by a software program. During the process, complex mathematical algorithms cause the substitution of numbers and letters for the original "plain text." The resulting cipher or coded message is in nonrepeating substitute code. This code cannot be broken without a major investment in equipment and highly skilled experts. This kind of resource is unlikely to be found outside the intelligence services of the major world powers.

Most encryption will eventually be done by means of specially designed hardware or perhaps "chips," which could be installed inside devices such as personal workstations. Some encryption is done by software programs called into the processing activities of large computers. Generally, the overhead costs of such encryption are considered too high for common use.

Key management is critical. The "key" is the single code needed to reverse the encryption process and thus end up with the actual plain text message. If you lose the key, you lose the message. In some systems, the hardware manages the keys. In others, the security officer must control the keys, sometimes through special hardware such as light emitters. The ultimate goal of the scientists working on security systems is an encryption service totally controlled by a network security center. The keys would then be generated as needed, with primary keys used to identify the network units or nodes and secondary keys used to encrypt individual messages.

Economical encryption hardware, probably in the form of "chips," and practical network encryption centers are coming. Their arrival will depend on market demand, which so far has been only slight. The application of extensive personal workstation automation networks with resulting security vulnerabilities should increase demands for encryption and thus decrease unit costs.

RISK ANALYSIS

When complex situations are faced, especially when high-cost risks are involved, managers like to have some assurance other than instinct that the right course is being followed. In security situations, popular theory calls for a risk analysis. This process uses the mathematical theory of probability to arrive at data that are supposed to indicate proper courses of action and suitable levels of investment in security measures.

Unfortunately, we do not have the benefit of enough experience to be able to construct reliable probabilities. Our best results are, then, a series of estimates multiplied by guesses. The many theories, processes, computer programs, and other methods suggested in the computer press and touted by innumerable brochures all have fatal flaws. In an earlier book, *Managing Information Security—a Program for the Electronic Information Age,*[16] I discussed these flaws in detail.

Most critics say, "What is the alternative? After all, an estimate is better than nothing."

Well, yes and no. A risk analysis, carefully done on a very limited scope—say a single process or at most a single data system—and recognizing the fallibility of the resulting numbers, might be helpful in arriving at a decision. The risk analysis is a contribution to a wider decision process; it is not the process itself. Since most security situations involve imponderables and factors that cannot be converted to precise terms, good business judgment must prevail. In a recent situation, Lloyds of London gave an opinion that a major catastrophe in a data center carries a probability of once in five hundred years. The managers involved used that item as input to a decision process. Surely a large dose of management discretion must be used whenever a probability like that is entered to an equation.

The rational decision process on expending resources for security in PWA systems should be based on a set of decision rules. Examples of such rules might be

1. Determine information values and establish a cutoff level, i. e., don't expend security resources below a specified information value.
2. Set some reasonable information protection standards for places where PWA systems are in use, such as the re-

quirements to lock up tapes and disks, to protect documents, etc., in some logical manner.

3. Clearly identify valuable information elements in all forms.

4. Train and motivate people to think and act in a manner consistent with the business' best interests.

5. Perform risk analysis, knowing the fallacies inherent in the method, where especially difficult circumstances make rational decisions elusive. (Recall "risk management" theory from the foreword.)

6. Offer management alternatives so that security is seen to be a part of the business process—don't be afraid to counsel risk taking.

PRACTICAL APPLICATION OF THE SECURITY ELEMENTS IN A PWA SYSTEM

The security elements provided in a personal workstation automation system must be flexible enough to allow the user to select those required for a particular situation. In some cases, the organization may wish to enforce certain security minimums through mandatory security standards. This may be accomplished

- Through the system administrator, in which case a network of PWA units has a central control.
- By means of permanent software or hardware features installed in the system.
- By effective procedure implemented by manual or logical processes.

In any case, some portion of the security environment will be optional or selectable. For example, the system may provide automatic document marking and file protection indication when a user tells the system that a particular piece of information is of high value. The user must have the option to indicate various valuations or classification. Thus our first practical rule:

The PWA user must be able to select or reject security elements to meet individual circumstances or special security requirements.

Within the flexibility requirement are several special categories. One of these is access variation, which means that the user
must be able to specify gradations of access for different files. A
second application rule might be:

> *The user must be able to set up access limitations that will fit*
> *the working environment fairly precisely; e. g., the limitations*
> *match physical paper-file restrictions.*

As an example, the user may wish to have a file that can be
shared by those in his or her department, a file which is private to
the user, and a file which is available to the network or public.
The security elements in the PWA system should allow this arrangement without unusual difficulty. The reader should understand that such features are not unusually taxing in terms of
software or hardware—there are no technical reasons to prevent
such features.

A third rule is that user application of the security features
should be simple. No programming of tedious procedure should
be involved, to wit:

> *The user must be able to apply the necessary security element*
> *in the course of normal PWA system operation.*

Security elements of various kinds may have desirable characteristics to make them more reliable or more useable. Some of
these characteristics are:

- *Passwords.* These should be at least five to seven characters in length. The user should be able to change his or
  her password easily. No one other than the user should
  have the password. The passwords should be stored in
  encrypted form in the system. (Readers wishing more information about passwords should see *Modern Methods
  for Computer Security and Privacy,* Lance J. Hoffman,[5]
  Chapter 2, p. 6; Professor Hoffman explains the security
  implications of increasing password length.) Also, see Exhibit 11–1.

- *Maintenance.* The PWA system should allow the user to
  protect information while system maintenance is performed. Maintenance engineers may be able to access all
  files if security elements are breached while they are work-

EXHIBIT 11–1
Flexibility in Protecting Information—Variations in Using Logical Security Elements

Relative Security Provided/Cost	Identification	Logical Elements Applied	
		Authentication	Authorization
Least	Password 3-character	None	None
↑	Password 3-character	Password 3-character	None
	Password 6-character	Password 3-character	None
	Password 6-character	Handshake procedure[1]	None
	Password 6-character	Handshake procedure	Authority table[2]
↓ Most	Password 6-character	Physical profile[3]	Authority table

[1]In a handshaking arrangement, the computer uses some random number (such as the contents of the timing clock) to send the user an authentication number. The user applies a prearranged transform to the number. The transform is never shown in the system and is difficult to construct from a few examples.
[2]The completed authentication is matched against a table which contains the user's authorized activities. (This may include authorizations to see, move, extract, print, perform, modify, etc.) The user may be a program.
[3]Systems are available which recognize physical aspects or characteristics of the user, such as voice, fingerprints, hand geometry, etc.

ing on the hardware. The user should be able to control this situation. Incidentally, good system administration in all cases requires that maintenance activities be actively managed. Responsible managers should be aware of maintenance activity, why it is being done, by whom, etc.

- *Media.* Storage and control of tapes and disks should be a planned process, not merely a casual decision to throw some disks in a desk or cabinet. Inventory of media should be a routine occurrence.

- *Communications.* Hardware and cables association with communications control and connections should have security consistent with that provided to other parts of the system. Telephone company employees should not be allowed casual access. Communications rooms are critical information processing facilities and should be treated as such. Controllers and other network system devices must be given security equivalent to that provided a central computer center.

- *Printing.* PWA systems using central printing facilities should allow the sending user to specify "restricted" delivery. In such a case, the person creating a document to be printed centrally can cause the output paper to be deposited in a locked bin upon delivery, or printing can be suspended until the recipient arrives on the scene and enters a password or key.

- *Transformation or Encryption.* Highly sensitive information requires encryption to provide really reliable security. This is especially critical for transmission over public utility services. Users should be able to call for encryption through a simple routine. Unfortunately, development in such capabilities is still in the future. (In the interim, security managers must warn system users that data communications are insecure whenever transmissions move outside company-controlled spaces.)

STANDARD ACCESS PROCEDURES

Observation of some branch office operations in high-technology companies often leads to amazement. The clerical people are using several different PWA input and inquiry systems involving differing equipment. This means that the sign-on and access control procedures are unique in each case. The employees using these PWA systems must remember individual protocols and passwords. Separate systems may be in use for customer account inquiries, sales leads, service calls, personnel/payroll, supplies ordering, and orders status.

Most businesses have done a poor job of making access to these systems a standard, simple process. In fact, most have not yet addressed the matter. Computer manufacturers like to make systems processes unique—thus keeping customers from mixing brands. Unfortunately, even for the same manufacturer, different lines of equipment often have different protocols for access ("sign-on").

Charles Symons, systems security manager of Rank Xerox Ltd. in London, has suggested a standard sign-on protocol. In the application of such a standard, manufacturers bidding on equipment or systems requirements would be asked to provide facilities to meet a simple set of criteria. One such set might include:

- Passwords of seven characters, to be stored in encrypted form.
- Forced password changes at a frequency set by the user security officer.
- A system which denies repeat password use.
- Individual user identification of a standard type and length (could be a plastic card or voice recognition, fingerprint matching, etc).
- Temporary first-time passwords issuance by the system to be immediately replaced by a user-selected password.
- Standard system interface at sign-on time, e. g., greeting, password entry query, password blot-out, authentication query, etc.
- System standard reactions to improper or outdated answers to queries.
- Automatic system promptings related to security, e. g., last time signed on, reminder that password change is imminent, etc.

When confusing or complex access controls are in use, people will respond by writing down "how to sign on," and then posting the process on the wall or equipment. If we really wish to make improvements in security for widespread PWA accesses, we have to make the systems' protocols consistent. Symons offers the illustration of driving a motor car: In any country, there are the standard brake, clutch, throttle, and steering wheel, so anyone can get in and go without written instructions. Our security systems for personal workstations should be as easy. We should be able to learn how to use them once and then go.

FLEXIBILITY IN ELEMENT SELECTION

We have seen that security for PWA systems may be tailored to requirements by selecting a suitable combination of security elements from the physical, procedural, and logical sets of elements. The professional manager should understand this concept, for it will enable him or her to make correct decisions about the selection of security elements.

Taking the various elements one by one, we can suggest varying degrees of protection. Then, by using a chart, we can illustrate the effects of the possible combinations of elements. In each case, we will show the most rigorous protection on the left and the weakest on the right. Note that the weakest may be correct in some circumstances, either as a stand-alone element or in combination with other elements (Exhibit 11–2).

Within the various elements, there are ranges of effectiveness. A most appropriate illustration is the logical access control system, which consists of identification, authentication, and authorization subelements. Today, the most common identification element is the password. A password is an established string of characters, private to an authorized system user, which supports a claim to a specific identity.

The user enters the password into the PWA system, which then searches through a table of authorized passwords. If a match is found, the user is approved for access to the system.

Passwords may also be used to gain access to data files or to run programs. Computer security manager R. I. Petterson of Union Carbide suggests that, in such use, they be referred to as "lockwords." This is a good practice, as it clearly defines which

EXHIBIT 11–2
Variations in Security Element Applications

Least rigorous ←---→ Most rigorous

PHYSICAL ELEMENTS

Allow access only to group members	Allow access to department members	Restrict access to specific individuals

PROCEDURAL ELEMENTS

Tracking of active employees	Tracking of assignments	Monitoring of specific authorizations

LOGICAL ELEMENTS

Identification element only	Identification and authentication elements	Full access control

level of access one is discussing. Passwords may also be used in the authentication step (although a more rigorous token is preferred), when the system user proves that the identity claimed is genuine. As we will see, an effective level of protection requires that the password not be used for all access control steps.

Variations in protection quality (and costs) result from increasing the password or lockword length, from using elements other than passwords for the authentication step, and from providing specific see/change/run authorizations for each user. Exhibit 11–1 illustrates this phenomenon—that the protection level from an investment in security elements is almost infinitely variable. It also shows that we can almost always find another way when obstacles appear to our providing security for valuable and vulnerable information.

INFORMATION INTEGRITY, PRIVACY, AND SECURITY—A DEFINITION

The principles of logic are always of help in defining a task. We can submit that any task that is to be successfully completed must have boundaries. Without defined limitations, we could have a task that requires, "Make sure that nothing goes wrong in this company." (This *might* be the task of the company president, but even for that job the task definition is surely more precise, perhaps, "Set out policies and practices that will ensure effective operation.")

Setting out task boundaries is necessary for the performer to know what he or she is expected to do. Open-ended tasks that can be projected into general areas of responsibilities are impossible to accomplish. It is important that we understand precisely what it is we are expected to do so that our limited security resources will be expended wisely on the task itself and not on other jobs.

In the current literature and in discussions at meetings and seminars, there is confusion about the meaning and relationships among the terms *data integrity, data security,* and *data privacy.*

First, some definitions:

Integrity: The quality of accuracy and completeness, implying that the data have not been changed improperly, that the data truly reflect inputs, and that all expected data are present.

Privacy: The quality of being secure from observation by persons or systems outside the audience intended by the data owner—usually the person or business to whom the data belong.

Security: One of the elements necessary to ensure privacy or integrity; the combination of protective features needed to ensure freedom from unauthorized change, destruction, denial of access, or exposure to unauthorized people or systems.

Note that the qualities of *integrity* and *privacy* require more than security. They also require good systems design, proper procedures, effective supervision of data handling, establishment of policies and practices, and identification of information requiring special protection. Many of these requirements are basic management responsibilities and are not security elements. For example, the hiring, training, and direction of effective supervisors for a data entry operation is clearly not a security matter. Should the supervisors of the data entry operation become involved in fraud or other improper activity, that particular incident may be cause for security involvement. But general business operations procedures are the responsibility of the assigned operating manager.

The claim that human error is the most serious security problem is, therefore, fallacious reasoning. No doubt the integrity of data may be affected by poor procedure, inadequate training, ineffective supervision, or purposeful fraudulent actions. *Only the last* is a security matter. Should the security manager be asked to address data integrity or privacy problems resulting from bad system design, improper procedure, weak supervision, etc., the security job will become impossibly broad. Problems with human error, unless proven to be of fraudulent intent or sabotage, should be dealt with through the organization's systems analysis or audit and control resources.

It is fine to recognize that most data integrity and privacy problems occur through human error, but that fact serves to put security in its proper perspective. It does not make error a security responsibility.

THE PWA USER—KEY TO INFORMATION SECURITY

We have seen that there are plenty of opportunities for the users of personal workstation automation systems to violate good information security practice. For one thing, unless PWA users decide to apply good security habits as they work, the security elements that we have placed in the PWA systems will be worthless. Because these security elements must be responsive to business needs, they are necessarily flexible and selectable, i. e., the user may elect not to use them.

User training is most important to obtain optimum benefits from a business investment in PWA systems. We have seen the process by which a business determines the requirements for PWA and how a specific system is designed. A vital part of the installation process is, user training, which offers a golden opportunity to get our information security message across.

In essence, this message is, "*As a PWA system user you will be provided with a powerful information access and processing capability. You also will assume responsibility for protecting that information, which is a critical resource for our business.*"

This sounds pretty good, but people need continual telling and reminding. Among the alternatives for providing effective information security motivation are the following:

1. Security training modules by lecture or videotape which are included in the PWA system installation process; at Standard Oil (Ohio) such training is "built in" to the process of periodically reestablishing personal use authorizations.

2. Information protection training written into the self-instruction software provided to users with the PWA system. When the user wants to begin, he or she calls up a set of "how to use me" instructions on the VDT screen; security instructions will appear along with the details of how to run a program or create a document—this is a "best" method.

3. PWA system users are provided with a general-purpose information security pamphlet that contains an explanation of company policies on information security and specific instructions for the type of equipment involved. The user looks up the type of PWA system in use and finds the rules (see Appendix C).

4. Periodic security training or motivation sessions for security coordinators or other employees with security responsibilities can include special sections about personal workstation automation. Remember that the traditional approach used in the data center is not appropriate here.

We must reach and motivate the individual PWA user, who is the system operator, supervisor, and programmer all rolled into one.

5. Posters and reminders (things like rulers, folders, paper clip holders with security messages) are useful in keeping people aware. Effective security requires motivation, which cannot be achieved without a solid program foundation, so we need to look on posters and giveaways as a supplement to training, not a substitute.

The framework discussed in Chapter 4 is critical to providing an effective training and motivation atmosphere. Unless top management supports the information security effort with obvious intent, through published policy, motivation is "swimming against the stream"—you won't make much progress.[16]

Appendix C provides a sample PWA user security guide. The same materials can be used to make up posters.

12

Examples of Application of Security Elements in Personal Workstation Automation Systems

---

The variety of configurations, purposes, and system designs in personal workstation automation systems (as described in Chapters 5 and 6) prevents giving recipe-type instructions for securing information in such systems. Because many people have asked for illustrations of exact security element applications, we will illustrate some PWA systems we know about and comment on the use of security elements in those cases. The reader must accept, however, that these illustrations are only examples and cannot be transferred to other circumstances without careful analysis of particular requirements.

EXAMPLE 1

This application involves a powerful word processor with disk data storage and communications facilities. The equipment configuration is shown in Exhibit 12–1. The numbers refer to the security elements found in the three security levels, e. g.,

- Level 1   Physical security elements
- Level 2   Procedural security elements
- Level 3   Logical security elements (hardware and software)

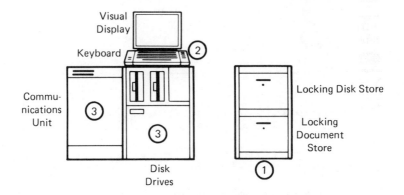

EXHIBIT 12–1.   Example 1: Wordprocessor/Communicator.

The particular system in Example 1 is used for document creation. The communications feature allows the managers serviced to send in drafts of memos, reports, etc., from home or from travel locations.

Security elements provided for this system consist of:

- From Level 1:   Secure storage for disks and documents in locking containers.
- From Level 2:   Marking and handling procedures for all files and documents classified as needing protection. Documents are marked through stamping; electronic files are marked through special headers or key-entered indicia on VDT (video screen) layouts.
- From Level 3:   The communications (message) system provides for information classification file headers that warn the recipient and prevent a broadcast message. All information in the message system is protected by passwords and file names.

EXAMPLE 2

This PWA system is a manager's professional workstation, used by a computer technologist who also has significant staff responsibilities at the corporate level. This system configuration is illustrated in Exhibit 12–2. Again, the numbers indicate use of security elements from the three levels.

Example 2   *111*

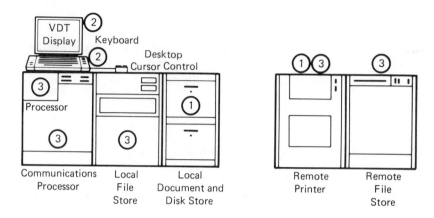

EXHIBIT 12–2. Example 2: Manager's Workstation.

This PWA system is connected to a high-speed coaxial channel, which allows the use of special attached units such as a communications controller, to give access to outside networks; a print server, to provide high-quality graphics and printing; and a central file store, where large volumes of information can be held in electronic form.

The user manager sends messages to about one hundred different stations, some as far as 5000 miles distant; creates documents and prints them, including graphics; and stores volume files. Documents are transferred among various workstations on the local network and on foreign (telephone-wire-connected distant) networks or individual computers.

Security elements used in this application include:

- From Level 1:   Disk storage cabinets and document storage facilities in the manager's office.
- From Level 2:   Document marking and handling procedures. Documents may be stamped or, if in "soft" electronic form, marked with a stored, program-generated security logo.
- From Level 3:   Messages can be appended with a security header, which provides warning to recipients and limits broadcast and retransmission. Documents can carry a security flag. Information stored on the central electronic file can be placed in any of three types of "file drawers" (electronic, not physical): public files, private files, or

shared files. In this last case, specific "other persons" may be listed in the security software as having authority to open the shared files. All files in electronic form are protected by passwords; security for files on the manager's office disk depends on physical protection, as the password system is not reliable.

EXAMPLE 3

This system consists of a desktop microcomputer with disk drives and printer. It is used by a manager to perform routine administrative tasks, including document preparation (drafts), message services on two networks, and storage of address lists, references, etc. It has a configuration as shown in Exhibit 12–3, with security element levels applied as indicated.

- Level 1 security elements: In this case, the user has secure storage for the disks containing local files. Document storage is also provided.
- Level 2 security elements: Document marking and handling procedures are in place.
- Level 3 security elements: Limited storage is available on the central storage disks of the message computers. These files are protected by passwords. Message security header flags are available along with message markings on the electronically generated message systems.

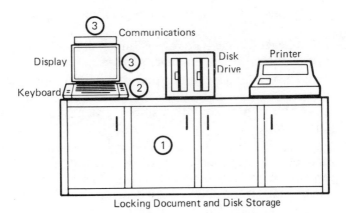

EXHIBIT 12–3. Example 3: Desktop Microcomputer.

Example 4   *113*

The reader may notice that none of these systems offers encryption, a serious shortcoming. These systems cannot safely be used to transmit highly sensitive information, although it can be created locally and printed out, and the electronic forms can then be erased. The documents then are handled appropriately, perhaps being transmitted by registered mail.

EXAMPLE 4

A minicomputer document processing system with several terminals is used to set up financial reports and to allow review and analysis prior to management use. This system has no network interfaces. (See Exhibit 12–4.) Input is by means of keying from other documents.

- Level 1 elements: Screening of display VDTs so that casual passers-by cannot read information. Special secure rooms for disk drives, processor, and printers. Document storage facilities.
- Level 2 elements: Document handling and marking procedures. Documents are marked by stamping.
- Level 3 elements: Files on disk are password-protected, but only to one level, so disks, like documents, must be locked up.

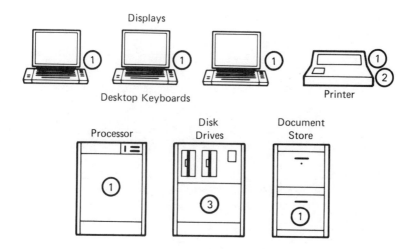

EXHIBIT 12–4. Example 4: Special-purpose Minicomputer.

Managers should use examples such as these, which have some evident shortcomings, as a guide to intelligent questions to be asked when planning for security of PWA systems in a particular circumstance. Some imagination and a constant awareness of the potentials for alternatives are required. The various security elements can be mixed and matched to fit any situation in tune with the business operation and the security budget.

13

Too Late

Some readers will now be saying, "But my company is too far along in automating personal workstations—if only I had read this book a year ago." If you are one of those people, welcome to the group!

Don't give up yet; although retrofitting security into already established PWA systems can be difficult, it is possible to achieve some minimal but acceptable security after the fact.

THE SYSTEMS SECURITY SURVEY

The first requirement before we can begin to evaluate the situation is to determine the information values involved. That is, we must have established information classifications so that we will know what must be protected and to what extent. Remember, the "work factor" set by the depth and quality of our security elements, used in combination, must be suitable to the information value that we have established. (Go back to Chapters 2 and 3 and read the parts about information valuation and protection if you are confused by this last statement.)

Having set a means for determining information value, we are ready to survey the PWA systems in place. We want to find out

1. What information is being processed (the single most important bit of information we need) and its value (classification).

2. Whether communications systems are used to transmit data: (a) inside the building or (b) outside, where public utility systems must be used. As we have seen, (a) is a different kettle of fish from (b) (Chapter 8).

3. Where information change of form takes place. That is, where is information entered into the systems, and where does it get printed out or displayed?

4. What media (tapes, disks) are used, and how are these media stored and accounted for?

5. If information files are stored on media permanently mounted in the device or in the system's "memory," are users able to prevent unauthorized persons from accessing that information?

From the answers to these questions we can assemble a crude description of the PWA system environment in our company and then begin to identify the corrective security measures needed. The chart in Exhibit 13–1 shows the process we should use.

EXHIBIT 13–1
Survey of Existing Personal Workstation Automation

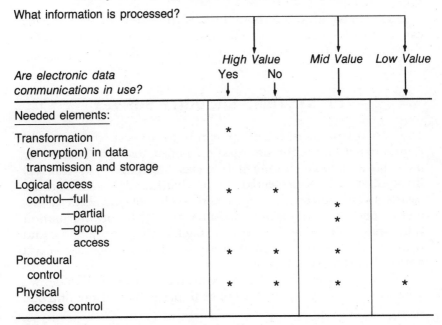

What information is processed?	High Value Yes	High Value No	Mid Value	Low Value
Are electronic data communications in use?				
Needed elements:				
Transformation (encryption) in data transmission and storage	*			
Logical access control—full	*	*		
—partial			*	
—group access			*	
Procedural control	*	*	*	
Physical access control	*	*	*	*

Epilogue

The concepts and ideas presented in this text are being tested in real-life applications in several advanced-technology companies. At this point in the development and use of personal workstation automation systems, the key elements to successful control and protection of electronic information seem to be

1. The concept of "information management" throughout the business operations.
2. The relationships among the information manager, the security manager, and the PWA systems users and implementation staff.

It is too soon to be able to report that a particular course of action is best among alternatives. But it is absolutely clear that, unless a business gets control of its information, those data will soon be in the public's hands.

In most companies, there is currently a void—perhaps unrecognized or simply not filled because of uncertainty—in the responsibility for managing business information. As we have seen, information is considered to be the key resource for business in the "information age"—the 1980s and 1990s.

The professional security manager owes it to his or her career to step into this void, to work with appropriate information (systems?) managers and system users to gain control *now*, before the interconnection of people via electronic information processors makes action too little, too late. Every business manager needs to be aware of "information asset" protection requirements.

There is not much time; this book was written with a PWA microcomputer with automated network connections. When will you get your new PWA system? Probably sooner than you think.

Appendix A

Policy

POLICY FOR INFORMATION SECURITY
ABC COMPANY

Effective: 1 June 19xx

TITLE: PROTECTING INFORMATION

<u>PURPOSE:</u>   All information used in our business is an asset, and as such must be protected from improper or unauthorized exposure, changes, or destruction.

<u>POLICY:</u>   All business information shall be classified in one of the following categories. The originator of business information is responsible for making a classification decision. General rulings on classification of information shall be made by the appropriate functional vice president (i. e., the function which budgets for information services in the relevant area).

Classifications are

1. RESTRICTED: Information of highest value, which if exposed or damaged, could result in serious consequences to profitability or operability.
2. Business CONFIDENTIAL: Information of value which, if exposed or damaged, could result in interference with operations or plans.
3. PERSONAL: Information regarding employees, ex-employees, or job applicants that individuals would normally wish to have protected in the interest of privacy.
4. ALL OTHER: Considered private to the company unless published, e. g., in booklets, advertising, public announcements, etc.

PRACTICES: Classified information is to be restricted in use in all forms (e. g., oral, paper, electronic) as follows:

1. RESTRICTED: Limited to those people specified in writing by the originator; may not be copied or transmitted to distribution lists electronically.
2. CONFIDENTIAL and PERSONAL: Limited to those employees having a specific need to know by virtue of job assignments, and to those specified by Vice President, Personnel.

Appendix B

Standard

PROTECTING COMPUTER INFORMATION SYSTEMS

Objective

To ensure the security of information processed electronically.

Requirement

Levels of Security

1. Physical protection. This includes facility access control, use of restricted areas, employee identifications, etc.
2. Procedural security. This includes proper separation of duties; control over changes to systems, programs, and files; system installation procedure; etc.
3. Logical security. Access control systems, operating system security features, special software packages, etc. Control must include user identification, authentication, and authorization. (See the glossary in Chapter 1 for definitions.)

When passwords are used for identification or authentication, they must be

1. Classified and protected in the same way as the highest classification of the information shielded.
2. Protected by overprinting, display suppression, or similar means when in use at a terminal or system device.
3. Difficult to guess.
4. Changed at a frequency appropriate to the local situation and information classification.

Access authorizations must change when job assignments change.

Authorizations must change to meet business situations.

Records of the activities above must be kept.

Use.   A combination of protective elements shall be used to provide security.

Marking.   Classified information must be marked.

Printed output.   Each page of a classified document must be numbered and the last page so noted, i. e., some type of marking or words to indicate that it is the last page. Each page, and the front and back covers, must be marked:

```
******************************
*          RESTRICTED        *
******************************

******************************
*         CONFIDENTIAL       *
******************************

******************************
*           PERSONAL         *
******************************
```

Exceptions.   Upon determining that extraordinary difficulty and cost would be incurred in meeting the requirements of the standard, exceptions may be approved by appropriate vice president and security manager, supported by a formal risk analysis.

Display screens.   Must include classification marking.

Responsibility. Managers shall use the security elements in combination to provide multiple defenses through which an attacker must progress.

Managers shall include a monitoring facility.

PERSONAL WORKSTATION SECURITY (OFFICE SYSTEMS, MICROCOMPUTERS, ETC.)

Objective

To ensure that business information will remain secure when transmitted and processed in minicomputers, computer and telecommunications terminals, and similar devices.

Requirements

1. Provide employee users with specific detailed instructions on the identification, marking, and handling of information. Processing of multiple unclassified files may result in classified information.
2. Place displays so as to prevent casual observation.
3. Establish, or use, available access control systems, management controls, and administrative procedures to:

   a. Limit employee access to information in electronic systems to that required by virtue of job assignments.

   b. Specify those actions which authorized individual employees may take (e. g., read only, update, modify, execute program).

   c. Monitor compliance with such procedure.
4. Protect and control all magnetic media by means of physical identification and the provision of secure storage.
5. When reports are to be printed from files via a remote terminal, the terminal operator must be alerted and prepared to provide required marking and protection.
6. Where minicomputers located in office-type situations provide a centralized processing and/or data storage facility for a distributed processing network:

   a. Physical access controls must limit entry to the computer area to those employees or vendor personnel specifically authorized access.

   b. Managers must control and approve:
- Operating system maintenance.
- Hardware maintenance.
- Initial processor loading (or equivalent).
- Setting of system clocks.
- Changes to operating documentation (such as runbooks).

Logs. All systems logs, console logs, etc., must be sequentially numbered to ensure an auditable record of all operator actions.

Appendix C

Booklet for Employees
Using
Personal Workstation
Automation Systems

If you use:

- Word processors
- Electronic typing systems
- Professional workstations
- Computer terminals
- Minicomputers
- Copiers, facsimile machines, printers

this booklet is for you.

This booklet is designed to help the user of a personal electronic workstation to protect our business information.

Information which requires special protection has been defined in a Policy XXX, which helps managers indicate information values.

Your Security Coordinator can help you if you should have further questions.

Our business information is always confidential until officially released. A "classification" indicates information which needs special protection.

"Classifying" is the responsibility of the originator of the information.

Our classifications are

- **Restricted:** Disclosure could cause serious damage to the company.
- **Business confidential:** Disclosure could have a damaging effect on the company.
- **Personal:** Disclosure might be embarrassing or harmful to the individual.

For each classification, special protective measures are required:

RESTRICTED

- All documents must be marked.
- Copy number and recipients must be recorded.
- Transmission in electronic form requires encryption.
- Storage requires the use of a safe or a heavy-duty file cabinet with bar lock.
- All documents must be double-wrapped for mailing.

BUSINESS CONFIDENTIAL

- All documents must be marked.
- All paper, tapes, disks, and cartridges must be locked in desk or file cabinet when not attended.

PERSONAL

- All documents must be marked.
- Information must be protected from unauthorized observation and kept in locked desk or file when unattended.

The printed form of classified information must be stamped to show classification.

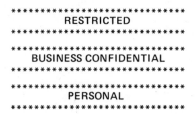

Or, if output is via electronic printer, the following markings should be generated:

```
******************************
         RESTRICTED
******************************

******************************
    BUSINESS CONFIDENTIAL
******************************

******************************
         PERSONAL
******************************
```

Our business information is a critical asset and may require special protection when in electronic mode.

Electronic systems may expose business information to improper use, destruction, or change, which could compromise our business effectiveness.

The distribution of classified information is based on "need to know."

What to Do—General

- Mark and handle all document output properly.
- Protect VDT displays of classified information from casual observation.
- Lock up disks, tapes, or cartridges containing classified information just as you would lock up the printed form of the same information.

- Arrange for "stand by" at an output printer to ensure immediate pickup of printouts if classified.
- If you store classified data on a file server, establish protections so that only you can access those files.
- Do not transmit Restricted data outside your local net, either to printers or to file servers, unless encrypted.
- Do not permanently store Restricted information on machines using disks which are not removable.
- Know your local security coordinator. Ask questions when in doubt.

Special Instructions

The following sections provide special instructions for users of specific types of electronic information systems.

<u>Page</u>

- Workstations
- Minicomputers
- Computer terminals
- Facsimile and copiers
- Teletype and electronic message systems

PROFESSIONAL WORKSTATIONS

Those who use personal machines and disks should follow "clean disk" practices! Security depends on careful management of files and access controls.

- Choose a password that is at least six characters long and not easily guessed; do not reveal it to anyone.
- Change your password periodically.
- Do not write your password down or store it in system files.

MINICOMPUTERS AND TERMINALS

A combination of security elements to protect computer-processed information may be selected from:

- Physical protections
- Procedural protections
- Software and hardware systems

MINICOMPUTERS AND TERMINALS

The elements selected must combine to offer protection suitable for the classification of the information being processed.

Our data center provides users with a range of security systems and can explain these security services to you.

Minicomputers located outside data centers to provide a centralized processing and/or data storage facility for a network must be protected by:

- Physical access controls to limit entry to the computer area.
- Positive management control over
  - — System maintenance
  - — Hardware maintenance
  - — Processor loading
  - — Setting system clocks
  - — Documentation change

Console logs, etc., must be controlled to ensure an auditable record of all actions.

COPIERS AND FACSIMILE

Communicating copiers and facsimile transmission devices are information systems that use facsimile images rather than character-by-character as a transmission mode. Nevertheless, the machines are electronic information processing devices.

- Protect all classified documents per Policy XXX.
- Ensure that receiving machines are in a secured area or that addressee is "standing by" when transmitting classified documents.
- Restricted information may be sent via facsimile or communicating copier only if:
  1. Identity of receiving operator is positively established.
  2. Copies are protected at all times.
  3. Information is sent to one addressee only.

TELETYPE AND ELECTRONIC MESSAGE SYSTEMS

Telegraphic systems and other basic keyed, wire systems are insecure for classified information. This vulnerability results from the retransmission via key entry typical of most such systems.

Electronic message systems that have security features available for marking and restricting distribution are considered secure except for Restricted information.

Your Security Coordinator is

_____

extension _____

Appendix D

PWA Security Checklist

CHECKLIST FOR SECURITY IN USING PERSONAL WORKSTATION AUTOMATION

1. Was this PWA unit or system installed after a formal analysis or study which included information security considerations?

   Yes _____ (Skip to Question 4.)
   No _____ (Continue with Question 2.)

2. Is the information processed or developed on this PWA system of critical import to the business? (Is or should it be classified for special care and control?)

   Yes _____ (Continue with Question 3.)
   No _____ (Skip to Question 4.)

3. Have rules and practices been established to protect this critical information when in paper or oral form?

Yes _____

No _____ (You need to establish a means for identifying information needing protection and to specify the means for such protection. This applies to the information in any form—paper, oral, electronic.)

4. Have PWA system users been instruction as to their responsibilities for protection of classified information in all forms?

Yes _____

No _____ (Motivation and training are essential to effecting information security.)

5. Are document handling procedures published for the control of classified information?

Yes _____

No _____ (These are needed to ensure consistency.)

6. Are media (tapes, disks) handling procedures established?

Yes _____

No _____ (These are required to ensure information integrity and security.)

7. Do PWA system installations include equipment (file cabinets, etc.) that will allow secure storage of documents and media?

Yes _____

No _____ (Information in any form is susceptible to theft.)

8. Are PWA visual display screens blocked from the view of passers-by if critical confidential information is to be processed?

Yes _____

No _____ (Most information compromise is via a company's own employees.)

9. Does PWA system software include file and message access control(s) that are rigorous (e. g., effectively block out any system user except those authorized to see that particular message or file)?

Yes _____

No _____ (If no access authorization is specified by user, default must be "none.")

10. Are system users aware of the difference between internal network security and external (i. e., public utility) network security?

Yes _____

No _____ (External networks are subject to activities beyond your control, such as copying or monitoring of traffic.)

11. Do printers or facsimile communications units in general service areas provide means for handling classified reports in a controlled manner?

Yes _____

No _____ (Reports or messages may be delivered to a central station automatically; means should be provided to prevent casual reading by passers-by or unauthorized persons.)

12. Have PWA users been instructed on the use of broadcast or multiple-addressee messages or documents?

Yes _____

No _____ (If high-value information is processed, multiple-address transmissions should not be permitted.)

13. Are PWA system/network security administration responsibilities formally defined and assigned?

Yes _____

No _____ (Logical or procedural security elements are
only as good as the administration which ensures their
currency and alignment with employee assignments and
management's need-to-know decisions.)

14. Have professional employees using PWA systems been
given instructions on the identification, marking, and
control of high-value original information sets developed
via PWA from noncritical data?

Yes _____

No _____ (Nonprotected information may generate
high-value competitive information after processing on a
personal computer.)

15. Are all employees provided with a continuing security
awareness program through area or department "security coordinators?"

Yes _____

No _____ (Individual acceptance of security responsibility is crucial where PWA systems are in use.)

16. Are PWA work areas and general office, laboratory, and
engineering areas given regular inspections to ensure
compliance with rules governing protection of information?

Yes _____

No _____ (Regular inspection reports sent to responsible supervisors ensure continuing protection.)

17. Where PWA system design does not provide acceptable
controls on access to files or messages, have alternative
security measures been adopted?

Yes _____

No _____ (If software security is ineffective, valuable classified information should be stored on a tape or disk and removed from the system when not in use.)

18. Have security practices been established and enforced covering communications elements, e. g., coaxial cables, telephone switching rooms, cable drops, etc.?

Yes _____

No _____ (Communications hardware is vulnerable.)

References

1. *The Seybold Report*, Vol. 10, No. 16 (April 27, 1982). Media, PA: Seybold Publications, page 16–3.

2. Mark L. Gillenson, "The State of Practice of Data Administration," *Communications of the ACM* (October, 1982), page 699.

3. *EDP Analyzer*, Vol. 19, No. 1 (January, 1981), "Coming Impact of New Technology," page 10.

4. John M. Carroll, *Computer Security*. Los Angeles, CA: Security World Publishing Company, 1977, pages 95–109.

5. Lance J. Hoffman, *Modern Methods for Computer Security and Privacy*. Englewood Cliffs, NJ: Prentice-Hall, Inc., 1977, pages 1–54.

6. Charles L. Howe, *Datamation*, Vol. 28, No. 1 (January, 1982), "Coping with Computer Criminals," page 118.

7. Practical Office Automation, *EDP Analyzer*, Vol. 20, No. 1 (January, 1982), Canning Publications, Vista, CA, page 8, et al.

8. James A. Schweitzer, *Security Management* (December, 1980), "Policy Structure gives the basis for an Effective Security Program."

9. *The Seybold Report,* Vol. 10, No. 16 (April 27, 1982) "Xerox's Star." Media, PA: Seybold Publications, Inc.

10. John Diebold, *Infosystems* (October, 1979), "IRM—New Directions in Management," page 41.

11. Brandt Allen, Darden School Working Paper (November 9, 1981), University of Virginia.

12. William R. Synnott and William H. Gruber, *Information Resource Management.* New York: John Wiley & Sons, 1981, page 12.

13. Chris Edwards, "Security for Your Microcomputer," *Management Accounting* (April, 1980), p. 37.

14. Leslie D. Ball, "Information Security in the Automated Office," Datapro Research Facilities Management report A39-500-201, July, 1981.

15. Charles Symons, Rank Xerox, Ltd.

16. James A. Schweitzer, *Managing Information Security—A Program for the Electronic Information Age.* Woburn, MA: Butterworth Publishers, 1982, page 50.

17. John A. Shoch and Jon A. Hupp, "The Worm Programs—Early Experience with a Distributed Computation," *Communications of the ACM;* Vol. 25, No. 3, March 1982. Copyright 1982 by the Association for Computing Machinery, Inc.

18. James H. Carlisle, "The Automated Office: Making it Productive for Tomorrow's Manager," *Administrative Management,* January, 1981.

19. "Productivity—Challenge of the 80s," American Productivity Center, Houston, TX and Office of the Future, Guttenberg, NJ; Report, 1981.

20. Reprinted by permission of the *Harvard Business Review.* Excerpt from "Catching up with the computer revolution," by Lynn M. Salerno (November–December 1981). Copyright © 1981 by the President and Fellows of Harvard College; all rights reserved.

21. Herbert S. Dordick, Helen G. Bradley, and Burt Nanus, *The Emerging Network Marketplace.* Norwood, NJ: ABLEX Publishing Corp., 1981, page 9.

22. Charles P. Lecht, "Our Computerized Future," *Telecommunications* (May, 1982), page 50.

23. James Martin, *Security Accuracy and Privacy in Computer Systems,* Englewood Cliffs, NJ: Prentice-Hall, Inc., 1973, page 3.

24. Leonard J. Krauss and Eileen MacGahan, *Computer Fraud and Countermeasures,* Englewood Cliffs, NJ: Prentice-Hall, Inc., 1979, page x.

25. Alan F. Westin, "Information Abuse and the Personal Computer," *Popular Computing* (August, 1982), pages 112–115.

26. Susan Chase, "Computer Companies Develop Devices to Ease Programming," *The Wall Street Journal* (June 25, 1982), page 21.

27. "Debate Over Office Networks," *The New York Times* (August 15, 1982), page F21.

28. "The Dawn of IRM," *Computer Decisions* (October, 1982), page 94.

29. James Martin, *Design and Strategy for Distributed Data Processing,* Englewood Cliffs, NJ: Prentice-Hall, Inc., 1981, pages 375–388.

Index

I

K

L

M